The Sleeping QUEEN

A challenging message for the Body of Christ, and I believe a timely one. Jesus is still the greatest liberator of women there has ever been. It's time to embrace His true mandate of women in leadership and the marketplace, and to align with God's word. We will not be effective until women are released into their full potential.

—**Mark Bilton**/ B.Sc, Grad.Dip.Bus, MBA. FAICD. FAIM, Founder of www.CalledToBusiness.com

Raw, soulful and candid…this book will take you behind the scenes of becoming a woman entrepreneur and what it means to stay connected to God and family while coming to terms with the often conflicting emotions that are an inevitable part of your entrepreneurial journey. A moving must-read!

—**Kendall SummerHawk**/Leading Expert in Women Entrepreneurs and Money

Bettina hits the proverbial nail on the head in addressing the lack of feminine leadership in the entrepreneurial world. Fortunately, we can find the world's first female investor in Proverbs 31: an entrepreneur who had her priorities in order. Read Bettina's work, learn and prosper!

—**Carolyn Castleberry**/Author of *Women, Take Charge of Your Money*

If you're looking for a modern-day example of the Proverbs 31 woman to be your next Best Friend, Bettina Langerfeldt is it! After devoting her life to raising and educating four children with her dear husband, she now teaches others, especially women, how to live a prosperous, productive life.

—**Rhea Perry**/Founder of EducatingforSuccess.com

The Sleeping
QUEEN

*The Divine Awakening of
the Entrepreneurial Woman*

BETTINA LANGERFELDT

New York

The Sleeping QUEEN
The Divine Awakening of the Entrepreneurial Woman

© 2017 BETTINA LANGERFELDT

Published in New York, New York, by Morgan James Publishing. Morgan James and The Entrepreneurial Publisher are trademarks of Morgan James, LLC. www.MorganJamesPublishing.com

The Morgan James Speakers Group can bring authors to your live event. For more information or to book an event visit The Morgan James Speakers Group at www.TheMorganJamesSpeakersGroup.com.

Shelfie

A **free** eBook edition is available with the purchase of this print book.

CLEARLY PRINT YOUR NAME ABOVE IN UPPER CASE

Instructions to claim your free eBook edition:
1. Download the Shelfie app for Android or iOS
2. Write your name in **UPPER CASE** above
3. Use the Shelfie app to submit a photo
4. Download your eBook to any device

ISBN 978-1-63047-898-8 paperback
ISBN 978-1-63047-899-5 eBook
ISBN 978-1-63047-900-8 hardcover
Library of Congress Control Number:
2015919720

Cover Design by:
Stephanie Delhey

Interior Design by:
Bonnie Bushman
The Whole Caboodle Graphic Design

In an effort to support local communities and raise awareness and funds, Morgan James Publishing donates a percentage of all book sales for the life of each book to Habitat for Humanity Peninsula and Greater Williamsburg.

Get involved today, visit
www.MorganJamesBuilds.com

Habitat
for Humanity®
Peninsula and
Greater Williamsburg
Building Partner

In loving memory of my father
Hans C. Langerfeldt

CONTENTS

ACKNOWLEDGMENTS

*There are a number of amazing people
without whom this book would never have happened.*

Ruth Klein
Thank you for believing in this project and for seeing what I could not
see: that I actually could write! Without your incredible support and
wise guidance I could never have written this book.

Ed Rampel
Thank you for the invaluable editing and for cunningly unravelling my
trilingual language knots!

Morgan And James Publishing House
Thank you for your amazing support and for making the practical side
of this book possible.

A Special Thank You

To my Savior, Lord and King, Jesus Christ

For your unfailing love, never-ending mercy, enabling grace and faithful guidance.

To my beloved husband, Robert

My soul mate and best buddy, you believed in me when even I myself couldn't. Thank you for your faithfulness to God and to me, your patience with this dreamer, your unfailing support and encouragement, and for always keeping my feet on the ground. I love you.

To our wonderful children

My precious treasures, Sabine, Stephanie, Thomas and Sophie. You were my inspiration for this project, as you taught me more about education and entrepreneurship than anybody else could ever have done. The greatest reward for me on earth is the honor to be your mom. With love, Momma!

To my Bible Teachers

Thank you to Andrew Wommack from Charis Bible College, and Arthur Meintjes from Kingdom Life Ministries, and many other faithful servants of God, for your generous impartation of the Word of God to me and to the world.

To my amazing Business Mentors

Who inspired me, spurred me on and taught me to navigate the marketplace without shipwrecking: Rhea Perry, Diana Fontanez and Kendall Summerhawk, Kailash Sozzani and Richard Shappiro.

To all the business women in the world

Who courageously face all odds to step up to their divine calling of impacting lives with their creativity, expertise and talents. Your labor is not in vain. You are an agent of change for the future generations!

INTRODUCTION

Although it is has become more common to see women launch their own companies, statistics clearly show that the creativity and entrepreneurial potential of women is a largely underexploited source of economic growth worldwide. This tendency is even more evident in Christian circles.

There are still countless barriers holding women entrepreneurs back from fulfilling their promise as feminine leaders, so they can contribute fresh and creative business ideas, thereby creating new sources of prosperity for themselves and their community.

Some of these barriers are very evident and are a direct consequence of the historical discrimination women have been the victims of worldwide: less education, stereotypes and difficulties accessing financing and to networking.

Countries like Iceland, Finland and Norway have the lowest gender differences. Out of 142 countries, the USA is in 20th place after Germany, Switzerland and Canada. The Gender Gap is even more accentuated in Spanish-speaking countries: Spain ranks in 29th place, Mexico in 38th

place and Chile in 66th place. Iran, Syria and Yemen present the biggest Gender Breach. (Source: World Economic Forum, 2014.)

The World Bank's 2011 World Development Report suggests the productivity of some countries could increase by as much as 25% if discrimination against women disappeared.

This realization has spawned government programs promoting and supporting women who want to open their own companies, like the European Network of Female Entrepreneurship Ambassadors and European Network of Mentors for Women Entrepreneurs. Nevertheless, other barriers exist that are rarely addressed by government programs that assist feminine entrepreneurship:

Most often it is the woman herself who establishes hidden, but powerful obstacles that do not allow her to prosper once she goes into business and worse, cause her to never give herself the necessary permission to step into a feminine leadership role as a businesswomen, even when the doors of opportunity are wide open.

The main source of these barriers is a deeply engrained misconception about what true womanhood and entrepreneurship are really about. For example, very often it seems society accepts for an educated woman to open her own company, but at the same time, it's considered to be extremely unspiritual and greedy for her to pursue wealth and money.

The result is that the woman who receives the God-given calling to business constantly struggles to reconcile her inner drive to create wealth for herself and her family with the counterproductive shame, disdain and unworthiness she gets from herself and her environment.

Having to fight her way through a man's world adds to the dilemma of adopting masculine formulas for success that affect her inner feminine integrity. This lack of empowerment of the woman entrepreneur in society has huge consequences:

The lack of a sense of accomplishment triggers feelings of disappointment, unworthiness, anger and resentment in herself.

These emotions are reflected in her business, because they directly affect her level of leadership, the choice of her market niche, the amount she charges for her services, her marketing decisions, a diminished ability to set healthy boundaries that protect her time and finances, etc.

The ripple effects in the global economy are huge: less jobs and prosperity, less economic growth and a lower level of family wellbeing.

This book offers a fresh perspective on the role of the woman entrepreneur as a legitimate—and highly needed—leader in society and powerful contributor to the prosperity level of families, communities and economies worldwide. It unveils myths about feminine entrepreneurship that have been silently accepted for centuries and banished women to a place of little or no relevance in their society.

It also sheds new light on the spirituality of entrepreneurship, money and wealth creation by women and offers an eye-opening, biblical viewpoint of why women can and should fulfill their authentic role as feminine influencers, which is so badly needed.

The reader of this book will discover the amazing contribution a woman was created to make to society with her unique feminine gifting and the priceless enrichment her divine calling to the business world is meant to have. As you journey through these pages you'll experience how historical barriers that have deterred women for ages from engaging in successful feminine enterprises are exposed and broken.

The sleeping queen inside of you will awaken! Your mindset about true womanhood and female entrepreneurship will be powerfully renewed. You will feel inspired and released to confidently step into the God-given position of empowered leadership and wealth creation you were always meant to have.

— *Chapter 1* —
THE SLEEPING QUEEN
A Call to "Wake Up"!

I nés heard the phone ringing. She knew it was her mother. Inés' husband was on a business trip and she always called to see if everything was fine. Inés knew she meant well, but she noticed that lately her parents' excessive concern was irritating her more than usual.

When would they ever realize she was a grown up now? Inés was 35 years old, had three children and was perfectly capable of taking care of herself and her family, even when her husband was travelling.

Immediately she felt badly about her rebellious thoughts towards her parents. After all, they were loving and had always taken good care of her and her brothers. She sighed and dutifully answered the phone. Just as she had expected, her mother sounded worried. She and her father did not like the idea of her staying at home alone with her children, without a man in the house.

After reassuring her that all was well, Inés had to smile. She was always going to be their little girl! She wondered if her relationship to her daughter, Laura, would be that way once Laura was 35?

Her thoughts were interrupted as she glanced at her watch and saw it was time to go to work. As she drove down the highway to the corporation where she was a social worker, she could not help but notice she was bored. Ten years ago she had been passionate about helping people, but now her daily activities seemed like an endless routine she would work on mechanically every day. Her days at work had become a dreary ordeal to her. How long was she going to be able to do this?

Since her friend had invited her to that woman entrepreneur's meeting a few months ago, her outlook on life had shifted. That day she chatted with a coach and was astounded by her business model. Inés did not know business coaches could earn so much money by helping people! The concept blew her mind and stirred up something inside her that had been dormant for many years.

It dawned on Inés that she'd always wanted to have her own business, just like her dad. But that dream was somehow stifled during her teenage years and she chose to go to university instead, to study a profession in which she could pursue her dream of helping people. She had been a good student and her parents had been so proud of her back then!

But, after the entrepreneur meeting she saw a new door of opportunity open before her eyes: now she realized she could help many more people and earn more money if she had her own business as a coach. The very thought caused her to have goose pimples. It sounded so exciting!

She could already picture herself in an elegant office, talking with interesting people, helping them with problems affecting their lives. She was very good at listening and helping people solve their problems. Deep inside, she sensed she could be a fabulous coach!

What she mostly cherished was the idea of returning to her childhood dream of becoming a businesswoman. Her father was a successful businessman and had inspired all her brothers to become entrepreneurs, like him. He loved to talk about business opportunities all the time. Only a week ago, after the family dinner at her parents' house, all the men vividly discussed business, while she and the rest of the women washed the dishes.

She remembered when she was 10 years old and had proudly announced she was going to be a successful businesswoman when she grew up. Stating that she was going to open a restaurant, her father laughed at the idea. Inés' mother cuddled her, saying she was a princess who'd never need to do that.

A princess? That wasn't exactly what she felt like at her job! Being a businesswoman sounded much better to her, especially since she had discovered how she could use her talents to become a successful coach!

Suddenly Inés realized she had gone to college to please her parents and conform to the princess fantasy they had of her. In the meantime, all her brothers had built up successful businesses with the help of her father, but here she was, still complying with that little princess image all of them had labeled her with.

What would they say if she told them she was quitting her job and was going to start her own business? She cringed at the idea. She had grown up in a loving home and hated the thought of disappointing her parents.

Inés also knew that Rodrigo, her husband, would be supportive — but only if she could show him she was able to earn money with this new business venture. Now, why would he do that? She remembered she had never questioned his ability to make money when he opened his first company, years ago.

Fear struck her. At the entrepreneurial meeting she'd been so sure she had finally found her passion again, yet now Inés started to doubt that she would ever be able to earn enough money as a coach.

There was so much she had to learn! The coach she'd talked with had mentioned she would have to research a profitable niche, learn about marketing strategies to get clients, master the sales process, design her offers and set up business systems — the list went on and on.

Yet Inés felt it was something she had been yearning for all her life.

As she drove into her office parking space and saw the gloomy grey building she worked in, lurking over her like a dark prison, she made a promise to herself: somehow, she was going to get out of there! Whether everybody else liked it or not, she was going to educate herself as a coach and open the coaching business of her dreams.

As she crossed the threshold into the office building, her heart rejoiced. Her days in this place were numbered! She was going to leave this prison soon and pursue what she felt had always been God's purpose for her life!

And Inés was going to teach her little Laura that while now she was a beautiful princess, soon she'd become a full-fledged benevolent queen and empowered feminine leader. Just like her mom, Laura was not going to hide out, but was going to speak up and make an important contribution to her generation!

The Lack of Feminine Leadership and Entrepreneurship
Just like Inés, women around the world have evidently more to struggle with than men do when it comes to opening their own company or assuming leadership positions.

According to the ILO (International Labor Organization) in 2012, women occupy less than a third of CEO positions in companies and they are only one tenth of corporate directors. In the entrepreneurial arena it's not very different: only one fourth of contemporary U.S. companies are run by women.

Historically women have always been at a disadvantage compared to men, even when their qualifications exceed those of their male colleagues. According to the Global Entrepreneurship Monitor in 2012, women graduate from college with better qualifications, yet before they turn 30 years old women earn 10% less than men.

These statistics may not surprise you. Gender differences in the workplace and availability of economic opportunities is nothing new. Feminism and woman rights movements have made us aware for decades of these disparities and of the price women have to pay just because they are what French philosopher Simone de Beauvoir called "The Second Sex" in her 1949 book.

I have no intention to lean in that direction, as enough has been said about that by a lot of smart and well-meaning women who can speak more authoritatively on that subject than I can. My question simply is: are we aware of the price all of us pay when we give women less opportunity than men?

What Exactly Happens When Only Half a Country's Labor Force is Allowed to Develop Their Entrepreneurial Spirit?
According to findings of the European Commission's Small Business Act for Europe women account for only 34.4% of Europe's self-employed and suggests they need more encouragement in order to become entrepreneurs. The report states:

"This leaves considerable untapped human potential that is sorely needed to boost economic growth and create the new jobs required in today's difficult economic climate. If more women can be motivated to start up and lead companies, this could generate growth and jobs across the EU."

This is corroborated by the Organization for Economic Co-operation and Development, who devised the Gender, Institutions and Development Database, which measures the economic and political power of women in 162 countries (OECD, 2006). With few exceptions, the greater the power of women, the greater the country's economic success.

The World Bank's 2011 World Development Report suggests that in some economies productivity could increase 25% if the barriers due to discrimination against women were abolished.

Wow, 25%! What would that mean for every citizen of the planet? Even though things are changing, this lack of feminine leadership is not only affecting the wellbeing of women and of their families, but also the world's economies. Are we aware of this?

Is every well-meaning father, who does not believe women should assume leadership roles, aware that he might be depriving many people future job opportunities in a company his daughters might never found if they choose to listen to their dad?

Is every mother who does not dare to question the status quo, and keeps silent without voicing her opinion, aware of how this is robbing her daughter of the role model she desperately needs, so she can fully step into a future leadership position God has destined her for?

And what of the CEO who refuses to hire women for important positions in the company on the grounds that they are not as available as men are due to their family duties? Is he aware his short-sightedness affects the decision of thousands of women not to have children, which means there will be less taxpayers in the future who might sustain his old age?

Every time somebody tells a girl she cannot do something just because she is a female, doors of growth and opportunity for everybody close.

Although much has changed, little girls are still taught in very subtle ways by men and women alike they are not designed for leadership positions, but should instead submit to a supportive role second to a man's.

How Feminine Submissiveness is Engrained from Childhood

The story of Inés is the story of many women. The role women have to play in society is taught to them while they are still little girls. Children adopt a gender identity early on in life.

According to Ross Parke and Mary Gauvain in their book *Child Psychology: A Contemporary Viewpoint*, we find great consistency in standards of desirable gender-role behavior, both within and across different cultures. Males are expected to be independent, assertive and competitive; females to be more passive, sensitive and supportive. These beliefs have changed little over the past 20 years within the United State—and, apparently, around the world as well.

Although some cultures, like the Hispanic tradition, are more likely to highlight gender differences than others, there has been a historic tendency to put women into a submissive role.

In some cultures this is taken to such an extreme that women are not even allowed to eat at the table with the men or choose whom they want to marry. In contemporary Western civilization though, this subservient role for women is much more subtle. There is no obvious imposition, but as if they are on automatic pilot both men and women assume gender roles they have been taught and conditioned to adopt.

There is no wrong or right here. The only really important thing is that the woman is given a choice in the matter. I suggest we honestly answer the questions:

- Are these situations automatically imposed on her?
- Are these decisions disempowering her as a person who also potentially has an important process of personal development ahead of her?
- Are her interests and desires being respected and protected?

Young girls should be taught to be clear about what the gender role they want to step into really looks like before committing to a lasting relationship.

Most of them just adopt what society dictates and expect that, somehow, it will work out for them. Sadly, very often it doesn't, creating a growing number of lonely and disappointed women who refuse to ever submit and make themselves vulnerable to a man again. This all started with a wrong idea about feminine submission and what that really is.

Let's Talk About Submission

Submission is a big issue, especially because it's widely taught in Christian circles. It is a tricky concept, because it is presented by God Himself, yet seems to be very unattractive. Let's face it, nobody wants to be told to submit to another person. It goes against human nature.

Bible verses about submission have led to misinterpretations that have opened doors to abusive control of women for centuries. They have led women to believe they were pious if they tolerated a controlling husband, even to the point of physical abuse, or they have offended many women who have chosen not to follow the Christian faith, because these religious impositions seemed unfair to them.

If you, as an entrepreneurial woman, are confused about this topic and want to break free from the bondage of unfair subservience imposed on women that you yourself have been subjected to, it's crucial for you to get clear about this issue.

If your sense of identity as a businesswoman and your beliefs are not aligned with each other, then I can guarantee you'll hold yourself back from stepping into the leadership position God has called you to embrace, because that is exactly what happened to me.

After adopting a very passive role by submitting to my husband in all major family decisions it was extremely difficult for me to feel empowered as a businesswoman who had to make important decisions in my company. It took me years to fully step into the identity of a full-fledged entrepreneur who treated her business like a business, not like a hobby or pastime. So, let's take a close look at what the Bible says and shed some light upon verses about submission.

The Book of Ephesians 5, the polemic chapter about female submission, starts talking about general submissiveness in verse 21: "… submitting to one another in the fear of God."

This verse is followed by examples of how a woman should submit to a man, a child to his/her father and a slave to his/her master:

"Wives, submit to your own husbands, as to the Lord. For the husband is head of the wife, as also Christ is head of the church; and He is the Savior of the body. Therefore, just as the church is subject to Christ, so let the wives be to their own husbands in everything."

These verses can easily be misinterpreted, especially if they are taken out of context and used to exert power over women, totally violating what is written in the next verse:

"Husbands, love your wives, just as Christ also loved the church and gave Himself for her… So husbands ought to love their own wives as their own bodies; he who loves his wife loves himself. …Nevertheless let each one of you in particular so love his own wife as himself, and let the wife see that she respects her husband."

As you can see, the man is required to love his wife to the point of giving his life for her! This is a radical statement now and was even more so back then.

These verses were written at a time when women had no legal rights. Husbands could handle legal affairs in whatever way he chose to, without wives' consent. Men were also much more educated than women. Additionally, they also had the support of pagan philosophy, which viewed women as inferior forms of males.

These beliefs led to abuses that were very common back then, due to the excessive power of men over the almost nonexistent power of women.

Nowadays, in modern Western society, in which the man and woman have a more equal level of power, any argument can potentially become a power struggle in which none of the parties want to relinquish their position of authority.

That is why these verses are so important: they appeal to the attitudes of both men and women. One party is to respect and submit, but the other is required to give his life in benefit of the other. Viewed from this standpoint, submitting is the easier part, not the worst.

When both males and females comply with these verses, harmony within the couple and respect for each other's interests are guaranteed and no one's wellbeing is violated in order to benefit the other.

A woman can easily trust and therefore give her consent to a person who values her so deeply he would give his life to save hers. The problem nowadays is that women have witnessed too much manipulation and mistreatment and are not willing to make themselves vulnerable to a person who has taken advantage of them.

There is a huge difference between a submissiveness that's imposed and allows for abuse, versus full trust in response to a godly, sacrificial love.

The point is that you:

1. Understand the true meaning of biblical submission and how it's designed to benefit both man and woman alike, so they can live in harmony, with mutual respect for each other, as co-leaders and co-stewards of the resources and responsibilities God has given them.
2. Understand that being submissive is not equal to being passive and leaving the responsibility for making decisions in your

husband's hands. Help him! Educate yourself, develop and grow, so you can be a capable and experienced partner who can significantly contribute with her knowledge, experience and talents.

I hope that at this point you can clearly understand how God's true design for a relationship between man and woman has been twisted into a religious and legalistic imposition that has nothing to do with God and has done lots of harm to women for thousands of years.

Now you can hopefully also see how your lack of empowerment as a woman and therefore as an entrepreneur is the consequence of your upbringing, which has shaped your sense of identity and your beliefs.

The Powerful Synergy of Man Plus Woman

Once you become conscious of and understand how these cultural behavioral patterns have been deeply engrained in your mind and how they affect your decisions and the outcomes you achieve as a businesswoman, then you can change them.

In this book you'll find the necessary help and encouragement to go about making this change wisely. Many women are inspired by the modern day "Empowered Women Movement" and counter-react to the excessive control of men in their lives by entering into competition with them.

The result is an unnecessary power-struggle between both man and woman that drains their energy and forfeits the powerful synergy they were both created to live in by God Himself. Believe me, it's not about becoming more empowered as a woman—you're already as empowered as you will ever be. All you have to do is to connect to and go back to God's original plan for women!

Boy, Can She Reign!

Ironically, it is often the woman who is much more in charge than the man. Of course, it can be a character issue of the woman, but usually it's because either they live with a man who does not actively participate in running the home and educating the children, or they are left to raise a family entirely on their own.

Both of these scenarios are very typical, especially in the Hispanic culture. For example, in Mexico, 25% of the homes have a woman as head of the family and seven out of 10 active women are divorced.

These situations have given women no other choice but to face the odds and step into a position of empowerment many have not been culturally prepared for. They often start a new business out of need more than out of passion or as a result of the natural drive of an entrepreneurial spirit.

I am very familiar with the situation, because many of my clients fall into this category of courageous women who confront unfavorable circumstances in their lives with entrepreneurial creativity and resolve. They never cease to amaze me with their strength and determination.

The sacrificial spirit of an entrepreneurial woman who is struggling to provide for her family is phenomenal. A woman who fights for herself and for her loved ones is comparable to a lioness protecting her litter, even to the point of sacrificing herself.

If you're an entrepreneur who is the breadwinner of your home, let me pause and celebrate your courage and your resilience. Your position is not an easy one and I know you have been through some hard times!

But let me also encourage you. When you overcome the battles of life, you will always become a stronger and more confident person. For a woman entrepreneur, that experience is priceless. It will help you to face new battles with less fear and give you the stamina to endure hardships whenever they come your way again.

As you fight for yourself and loved ones, you're being a living witness of the power a woman is capable of displaying when she loves fiercely and with determination. As you courageously discover and use the strength God has given you, you're a role model for many women watching you and a powerful example for your daughters and granddaughters.

Most important of all is that you're aware of the fact that God loves you and is always with you. He is the perfect caretaker, provider and husband who will never control or take advantage of you.

Summary Chapter 1
The Sleeping Queen—A Call to "Wake Up"!

- Women struggle more than men do when it comes to opening their own company or assuming leadership positions. This lack of feminine leadership is not only affecting the wellbeing of women and of their families, but also the world's economies.
- The role women have to play in society is taught to them while they are still little girls. This causes them to be at a disadvantage when it comes to developing their leadership skills.
- Many Christian women have a wrong idea about feminine submission. This affects their sense of identity as a businesswoman and will hold them back from stepping into the leadership position God has called them to embrace,
- There is a huge difference between a submissiveness that's imposed and allows for abuse, versus full trust in response to a godly, sacrificial love. Man and woman were both created to complement each other by creating a powerful synergy.
- Courageous women who confront unfavorable circumstances in their lives with entrepreneurial creativity and resolve can always rest in God's unconditional love, favor and provision.

Powerful Action Step:

If you feel that the beliefs around womanhood that you grew up with are holding you back from fully stepping into your identity as a business woman, ask yourself:

As a business woman, what would I have to believe to be successful? For example:

- I believe God delights in my prosperity and gives me the ability to create wealth.
- I believe I have been called to touch many lives through my business.
- I believe that, as a woman, I am equipped with unique gifts and talents that will bring success to my business and my life.

Write down three to five new beliefs you want to adopt and journal how that will show up in your business.

— *Chapter 2* —

THE VIRTUOUS QUEEN
God's Plan for Feminine Leadership

T he day God revealed the virtuous woman to me was the same day I finally received the conviction that I was called to the business world. Until then God had been nudging me in that direction for almost half a year and I had resisted, resisted and resisted it.

In my eyes, that calling was not spiritual enough. I had business acquaintances who only seemed interested in acquiring wealth. It could not get any less spiritual than that!

No, that was not for me! I was going to help people solve some serious problems in their lives, like getting healed from sicknesses, receiving inner peace and joy by faith and cultivating a deep relationship with God.

But making money? How boring was that?

Besides, none of the people I admired for their spirituality were businesspeople. They were pastors, church leaders, Sunday school teachers and missionaries. I wanted to be like them. These people really had it all together when it came to being consecrated to God!

If there was a calling in my life, it would certainly be to have an eternal impact on people's lives, something that would transcend into heaven, forever and ever. Certainly not something that had to do with a topic as mundane as money and business!

Then she appeared! God knew exactly how to get me out of my religious mode and to open my mind to an age-old Truth that seems to have been buried under centuries of the accumulated dust of legalistic, religious teachings.

Legalism, man-made ideas about God, the influence of Eastern religions and their cultural background have undermined the role that God originally intended women to play in their societies.

I have honestly tried to dig under the layers of dust to show you what I believe is God's perspective on true womanhood. It's my prayer that this truth may liberate you from religious chains that have held you back from fully stepping into your feminine, God-ordained leadership role. In this Chapter, I want to invite you to journey with me through history, back to the primal, elemental and original idea of true womanhood.

But first I want to talk to you about the source of this information—the Bible—and why it has been a powerful foundation of my journey as a woman entrepreneur.

Please bear with me, as I am going to take you down a very brief, but profound philosophical trail that will give you more clarity and conviction. I want to talk to you about absolute and relative truths.

Why Absolute Truths are Valuable and Life-changing
The definition of relative truth: Truth that is true at only one time and at one place. It's true to some people and not to others. It's true now but it may not have been true in the past and it may not be again in the future; it's always subject to change and to the perspective of people.

The definition of absolute truth: Whatever is true at one time and at one place is true for all time and at all places. What is true for one person is true for all. Truth is true, whether we believe it or not. Truth is discovered or it is revealed, it is not invented by a culture or by men.

I know that nowadays it's very unpopular to state absolute truths when you talk about your beliefs. In the name of tolerance, we are taught to accept that every person can choose his or her own truth and belief system.

Of course this is correct and it's not at all my intention to violate this fundamental concept of personal freedom. But I do want to urge you to be very honest with yourself when you state your beliefs and what they are founded on.

If each person and culture can develop their own definition of what is right or wrong, then, basically, an act can be right for someone, even if it is cruel, hateful or harmful.

Therefore, culture or one's personal preference cannot dictate what is right or wrong. Neither can religion, for each region may have its own religion that was handed down to the people there from previous generations.

There must be a greater standard, one that is more correct and certain for us to live by. Otherwise we are left to invent our own opinions that will change in time, because of our culture.

A good example is the belief in mediaeval times that the Earth was flat. There was a time in history when this was adopted as truth and anybody who dared prove otherwise, like Galileo Galilei, was accused of heresy and severely punished.

I fear for people who adopt relative truths to live by. If everything is relative and whatever is good or evil depends on each person's point of view, how will you be able to distinguish between what is appropriate for your life and what isn't?

Playing around with good and evil on your own terms can be very dangerous, because you won't have a firm ground to make wise decisions on.

You have to find a trustworthy source of truth that is core to you and your beliefs, or else you will drift from one ideology to another, without ever having solid ground under your feet, upon which you can build something substantial for your life. Truth and falsehood cannot be questioned unless they have an ultimate standard. Most people, except atheists, believe God is that standard.

My Own Journey in Search for Truth

After a having made a long quest for truth, I find that the Christian world view is the most consistent with reality. I personally believe God's standard is taught in the Bible, and that the Bible is the Word of God. So, as a Christian I believe God determines what is true and that the Bible is his "instructions manual."

Although I don't have any intention to impose my beliefs on you, it's necessary that you understand the Bible is my source of truth and why this decision is pivotal in the discovery of the virtuous woman in my life as an individual and feminine entrepreneur.

When you adopt a truth as an absolute for your life, it becomes an irrevocable foundation for life-changing decisions you will make. It gives you solid ground on which you can confidently build your life, knowing and trusting nothing and nobody can ever pull that carpet out from under your feet.

In *The Book of Matthew*, Jesus explains that by heeding God's word, you are choosing a firm foundation to build a successful life upon:

"Therefore whoever hears these sayings of Mine, and does them, I will liken him to a wise man who built his house on the rock: and the rain descended, the floods came, and the winds blew and beat on that house; and it did not fall, for it was founded on the rock. But everyone who hears these sayings of Mine, and does not do them, will be like a foolish man who built his house on the sand: and the rain descended, the floods came, and the winds blew and beat on that house; and it fell. And great was its fall." (Matthew 7:24-27)

That is exactly what I have experienced with the proverbial virtuous woman, which became my truth for womanhood. When I discovered that she was the ultimate entrepreneur, I realized God Himself created women to be financially successful and that He has called each one of us ladies to be influential leaders in our communities, just like she was!

I finally recognized His plan for me and every woman on Earth: He wants us to be benevolent, wise and gracious leaders who have an important role to play in our society as a perfect complement to the leadership role assigned to men.

We are Queens Who Successfully Reign as Co-stewards of this World

As I stated in the previous chapter, one of the biggest barriers that keeps women worldwide from stepping into their role as feminine leaders is a wrong belief system about women and their place in society that has been prevalent in many cultures for hundreds and even thousands of years.

Manmade laws and regulations derived from wrong interpretations of biblical truths have kept women silent for far too long. It's time for us to go back to the quintessence of true womanhood that is masterfully described in *The Book of Proverbs*, written by King Solomon, more than 2,500 years ago.

The virtuous woman he describes in *Proverbs* 31 is assumed by many biblical scholars to refer to his mother, Queen Bathsheba. Solomon describes a woman who has perfectly fulfilled the feminine role of leadership in God's eyes: she was a full-fledged businesswoman and real estate investor who not only cared well for her family, but also made important contributions to society as a whole.

This shows us that, in God's eyes, women have a distinctive and important role to play in the world and are given full permission to divinely step into the leadership roles they were created for.

Let's go back to His plan for us and boldly claim our ground as legitimate leaders in contemporary society, not in competition with— or as an opposite to—man, but as gracious, wise and loving co-leaders willing to offer a badly needed feminine complement to a predominantly masculine-ruled world.

That's what Mrs. Virtuous woman did. Let's follow her example!

Are you ready to meet her? Dear Reader, according to *Proverbs 31:10-31*, here she is! (Drum roll, please!):

The Virtuous Woman

"10 Who can find a virtuous wife?

For her worth is far above rubies.

11 The heart of her husband safely trusts her;

So he will have no lack of gain.

12 She does him good and not evil

All the days of her life.

13 She seeks wool and flax,

And willingly works with her hands.

14 She is like the merchant ships,

She brings her food from afar.

15 She also rises while it is yet night,

And provides food for her household,

And a portion for her maidservants.

16 She considers a field and buys it;

From her profits she plants a vineyard.

17 She girds herself with strength,

And strengthens her arms.

18 She perceives that her merchandise is good,

And her lamp does not go out by night.

19 She stretches out her hands to the distaff,

And her hand holds the spindle.

20 She extends her hand to the poor,

Yes, she reaches out her hands to the needy.

21 She is not afraid of snow for her household,

For all her household is clothed with scarlet.

22 She makes tapestry for herself;

Her clothing is fine linen and purple.

23 Her husband is known in the gates,

When he sits among the elders of the land.

24 She makes linen garments and sells them,

And supplies sashes for the merchants.

25 Strength and honor are her clothing;

She shall rejoice in time to come.

26 She opens her mouth with wisdom,

And on her tongue is the law of kindness.

27 She watches over the ways of her household,

And does not eat the bread of idleness.

28 Her children rise up and call her blessed;

Her husband also, and he praises her:

29 "Many daughters have done well,

But you excel them all."

30 Charm is deceitful and beauty is passing,

But a woman who fears the Lord, she shall be praised.

31 Give her of the fruit of her hands,

And let her own works praise her in the gates."

God Gave You an Entrepreneurial Spirit!

If you have ever been criticized because you were different from other women due to your desire to open your own company, then you have to become best friends with the virtuous woman!

She was my source of comfort and strength during many times of doubt and delusion while I was on my own journey to become a businesswoman. Whenever I doubted myself or took flak from people who did not understand what I was doing, I could go back to these verses and connect with God's view of who I am and what my true identity is. This is what has kept me going for years, like a shining light that has illuminated even the darkest hours of my business journey.

It's fascinating how you can be acquainted with a Bible verse for years and then, suddenly, God gives you new insights that you had never realized before. I had studied the virtuous woman in numerous women's Bible studies, but had never seen this angle of her personality, which is so evident to me today.

The day God revealed the entrepreneurial virtuous woman to me I had come to the end of my rope in resisting God's call to the business arena. I had decided to fast and pray about it, trusting that he would somehow convince me once and for all that this was the right way to go. And He did!

I still remember it as if it were yesterday. I was finishing homework our pastor had assigned. We were studying Biblical finances and were asked to highlight every verse in *The Book of Proverbs* related to money, wealth and riches. (By the way, if you want to acquire solid financial wisdom for your life, read *The Book of Proverbs*—it's a timeless treasure you can glean godly wisdom from for every aspect of your life, not only for money matters!)

When I came to Chapter 31, the chapter of the virtuous woman, which I had read many times before, I highlighted and highlighted and highlighted the page. Almost every verse in that Chapter was related to money, riches and wealth!

It blew me away! Suddenly it became clear to me that God desired for women to be effective leaders and industrious businesswomen and that he desires for us to be super savvy with money.

I mean, this woman:

She was a trustworthy queen who diligently conducted the stewardship of the family budget with integrity:

"The heart of her husband safely trusts her; so he will have no lack of gain." (Verse 11)

She was an industrious queen who proactively embraced productivity:

"She seeks wool and flax, and willingly works with her hands.

"She stretches out her hands to the distaff, and her hand holds the spindle." (Verse 13 and 19)

She was a good steward-queen who applied solid business criteria to all of her money transactions, including providing for her household:

"She is like the merchant ships, she brings her food from afar." (Verse 14)

As a queen, she was a great manager. Although she had lots of servants, she was not self-indulgent or lazy, but loved working and took responsibility by providing abundantly for everybody who lived with her:

"She also rises while it is yet night, and provides food for her household, and a portion for her maidservants." (Verse 15)

She was a money-savvy queen, a full-fledged real estate investor and a wise businesswoman who knew how to create wealth by creatively multiplying her income:

"She considers a field and buys it; from her profits she plants a vineyard." (Verse 16)

She was a powerful queen conscious of her important role and responsibilities, so she took good care of herself and her body:

"She girds herself with strength, and strengthens her arms." (Verse 17)

She was a confident queen who knew what she was worth and was conscious of the huge value of her products. She did not shy away from additional work when it was necessary:

"She perceives that her merchandise is good, and her lamp does not go out by night." (Verse 18)

She was a very generous queen:

"She extends her hand to the poor, yes, she reaches out her hands to the needy." (Verse 20)

She was a queen of high standards who provided a secure and high quality lifestyle for her family:

"She is not afraid of snow for her household, for all her household is clothed with scarlet." (Verse 21)

You will love this one! She was an elegant queen who knew how to surround herself with beauty, she was creative with her clothes and had beautiful and expensive dresses:

"She makes tapestry for herself; her clothing is fine linen and purple." (Verse 22)

She was a creative queen, most probably a fashion statement in her time who created and sold clothes of her own design, which people were eager to buy and even to resell:

"She makes linen garments and sells them, and supplies sashes for the merchants." (Verse 24)

She was a dignified and strong queen, who confidently looked forward to the future with boldness:

"Strength and honor are her clothing; she shall rejoice in time to come." (Verse 25)

She was a wise and kind queen:

"She opens her mouth with wisdom, and on her tongue is the law of kindness." (Verse 26)

She was a faithful queen who took full responsibility for her loved ones:

"She watches over the ways of her household, and does not eat the bread of idleness." (Verse 27)

Verse 30 reveals the source of her unshakable wisdom and strength: God Himself!

The virtuous woman queen had a personal relationship with God:

"Charm is deceitful and beauty is passing,

But a woman who fears the Lord, she shall be praised." (Verse 30)

Isn't that the perfect picture of who every woman wants to be?

Do You Doubt You Could Ever Be Like Her?

This is where my preface about the absolute truth comes in handy. Do you remember the definition of an absolute truth?

"Whatever is true at one time and at one place is true at all times and at all places. What is true for one person is true for all. Truth is true whether we believe it or not. Truth is discovered or it is revealed, it is not invented by a culture or by religious men."

If you are willing to embrace the truth of God's word as an absolute for your life, on which you can securely construct your life upon, then nothing and nobody will ever be able to stand in your way of becoming an awesome virtuous woman queen!

By the way, this is what faith is all about! It's about believing firmly in something, even when you cannot see it yet!

Hudson Taylor, a famous missionary, said: "What is necessary, is not that we have a great faith, but rather that we have simple trust in God's great faithfulness."

If this is God's plan for us, then it is doable! Why would He set standards we could never reach? If a parent would require unreachable standards of his or her child we would find that to be unfair, even cruel and sadistic, wouldn't we?

Well, God is love. He is the perfect parent. He would never set standards we would not be able to reach.

This assurance is what kept me going when I did not resemble this lady at all. I resented her for being so perfect. Looking back I can say that, by His grace, I have grown to love her and to believe that I can grow into what she represents for us.

Women around the world have been kept in a delusion about what a woman is really supposed to look like. For many of us, our former female role models did not even resemble this lady. They did not take their position as feminine leaders in their society, because they did not know any better.

This book is a wake up call to all women who feel in their hearts that they were called to be like the virtuous woman queen and have an important contribution to make to this world, but who feel they lack the necessary support to step up and make it happen.

If you are surrounded by people who don't believe in you and your potential, you can find new strength from what I shared with you. Now you know that God believes in you and even created you as a woman who, in His eyes, can be a confident entrepreneur who never even questions her ability to be successful as a business woman.

Become an Agent of Change for the Future Generations

I'll take this even a step further:

Imagine what an influence the virtuous woman queen had on her daughters and her granddaughters! Wouldn't you have loved to be mentored by someone like her?

So, this is where I ask you: What legacy are we going to leave for the future generations, for our daughters, nieces and granddaughters?

Will we choose to keep silent for one more generation? Or will we boldly take a step to prepare a path for them, so they can go higher and further, to serve the next generation even better than we did?

Summary Chapter 2: The Virtuous Queen— God's Plan for Feminine Leadership

- When you adopt a truth as an absolute for your life, it becomes an irrevocable foundation for life-changing decisions you will make. An absolute truth is true for all time and at all places, whether we believe it or not.
- The virtuous woman from *The Book of Proverbs* shows us that, in God's eyes, women have a distinctive and important role to play in the world and are given full permission to divinely step into the leadership roles they were created for.
- If you are willing to embrace the truth of God's word as an absolute for your life, on which you can securely construct your

life upon, then nothing and nobody will ever be able to stand in your way of becoming an awesome virtuous woman queen!

- Women who choose to courageously step into their leadership role leave a legacy for the future generation of young women.

Powerful Action Step:

Mark 3 character traits of the Virtuous Woman that you most want to adopt in your life and answer my coaching questions that will help you make that happen. (Download my free workbook: "The Sleeping Queen's Workbook for Business Women" at www.TheQueensWorkbook.com)

Chapter 3

THE SPIRITUAL QUEEN
The Entrepreneurial Woman in God's Eyes

S usana was a passionate hairdresser who loved God with all her heart. She excelled at helping women to look beautiful and had an innate knack for giving each one of her clients the perfect haircut that suited her best. Her clients loved and recommended her to their friends.

Susana was thrilled. Her business was booming and every day she experienced how much her gifts brought happiness to her clients' lives. But she also wanted to increase her income. She dreamed of buying a beautiful home for her family and wanted to put aside money for her future. She also wanted to help her mother pay her medical expenses and realized she needed to earn more money to make that happen.

Since she had a very strong aesthetic sense she started offering her clients lessons on how to dress. They loved that too. Now Susana wasn't only helping them to improve their looks through hairstyles, but also giving them helpful tips on dressing attractively. Since her salon was always full of ladies and her calendar was fully booked during the week, she attended to the clients who wanted help with their wardrobe on weekends.

Everything went well until Susana started to feel very tired. She was doing what she loved, but began hating every moment of it. She felt trapped. Working more wasn't an option for growing her business and earning more money. Besides, she did not want to work more. Susana realized she also had other priorities in her life she'd neglected while running her small, but booming business.

Luckily, Susana had a friend who was a business coach and asked her for help. Her friend helped her discover a different niche opportunity that Susana had never considered before: She could successfully exploit her talents by becoming an image coach. All she had to do was redesign her offer and market to a different client who would be willing to pay much more for her services. That way Susana would be able to earn much more without working more.

The idea was perfect! A new door to a prosperous business opened and the possibilities of succeeding were huge, since Susana had always excelled at her profession. Now she could offer a high end service to businesswomen who wanted to improve their image and gain more visibility.

However, you'll be surprised to find out Susana cringed at the idea. There was one big problem she just couldn't ignore: Susana did not like businesswomen. In her eyes, they were superficial and selfish, only interested in making money and worst of all, were among the least spiritual people she had ever met.

Business and Spirituality: Two Opposite Journeys?
Susana's appreciation of businesspeople is not an exception to the norm. Most people see no connection between the messy, mundane marketplace and the purity and holiness of a spiritual life. The pursuit of wealth and the quest for more spiritual growth are seen as two opposite journeys.

This is how most people think when they consider business and spirituality to be mutually exclusive:

- Business is complicated and obscure. The quest for wealth creation is fueled by human selfishness and greed that can potentially lead to an unhappy life of shame and solitude.
- The spiritual path, however, will bring out the best in us. Lived to its fullest expression, it helps us to lead a fulfilled life that denies materialistic pursuits while focusing on serving others and to die according to our own desires.

Many businesspeople believe that too. Sometimes they don't even attempt to get interested in spirituality of any sorts, because they either don't feel "holy" enough, or they don't see how it could possibly connect with their interests.

Others compartmentalize their life. They might attend a church, but don't see how their business could ever benefit from that. On the contrary, they think they can "clean" themselves from the unholy business environment in which they've spent all week, by dedicating some of their time to God.

Even church leaders are biased when it comes to the different callings people seem to have in their life. They usually commend people dedicated to serving the church, which makes the rest of the congregation—those members "only" working outside of church—feel like second class citizens who are not as holy as the other "super saints."

In his book *Doing Business God's Way*, Dennis Peacocke asserts:

"The false teaching against material stewardship has had especially devastating results against the average Christian, who, unlike the pastor, is called to earn his living dealing with the material world. It has promoted a kind of 'second-class citizenship' in the Church. If you're spiritual, or 'called to the ministry,' you go fulltime into God's work. If not, you work in the fallen world, contribute where you can, and sometimes wonder why God didn't love you enough to let you be 'fulltime' and out from under the burden of the material world. At best you may become a deacon or Sunday school teacher, but you feel tainted by material things. At worst you become a 'cash cow' to the local church and are called upon to keep its projects running in the black."

The Entrepreneur in God's Eyes

It's interesting to note that this distinction so common in church is not made by God Himself at all. Old Testament patriarchs, like Abraham, Isaac and Jacob, plus many others, were avid businesspeople who certainly knew how to multiply their riches and prosper. They fully believed God was the One bestowing prosperity upon them! They knew that their success wasn't in spite of God but because of God.

These beliefs are prevalent amongst Jews up to this day. In his book *Thou Shall Prosper*, Rabbi Daniel Lapin provides an excellent 10-point resource of practical and spiritual wisdom found in the time-tested knowledge of the ancient Jewish faith and culture.

Many verses in the Bible clearly show how God Himself gives us the power to prosper in our lives, and that He delights in the prosperity of His servants. For example, just to name a few:

Deuteronomy 8:18 New King James Version:
"And you shall remember the Lord your God, for it is He who gives you power to get wealth, that He may establish His covenant which He swore to your fathers, as it is this day.
God will not only give us the ideas to create money, He will also show us how to achieve more income."

Isaiah 48:17 New King James Version:
"Thus says the Lord, your Redeemer,
The Holy One of Israel:
'I am the Lord your God,
Who teaches you to profit,
Who leads you by the way you should go.'"

Entrepreneurship is Godly and Spiritual

God Himself is passionately interested in getting involved in our material world. Since He is a spiritual being (*John* 4:24), he can only do that through us! This happens in many ways—and not only in the business arena.

The word "Entrepreneur" comes from the French and means:

"A person who organizes and manages any enterprise, especially a business, usually with considerable initiative and risk."

The key word in this phrase is "any." You can be an entrepreneur in any enterprise.

It might be a businessman or woman who establishes a business, but it can also be a missionary who ventures into Africa to build a hospital and spread the Word of God, or a philanthropic person who organizes a charitable organization raising funds for treating cancer in children.

The entrepreneurial spirit should be present in every endeavor of mankind, because it is part of our nature. God made us that way.

It is even applicable to an employee who embraces his or her tasks with self-initiative and creativity. That is what will make the job much more fun and bring many rewards to the worker, too. His employer will deeply appreciate this proactive attitude.

The world would be a different place if everybody would unleash their entrepreneurial spirit in whatever task they are dedicated to. To a higher or lesser degree, we all do that, because being creative and entrepreneurial is part of human nature.

Genesis 1:28 says we are made in the image of God—and God is a mega-entrepreneur. He is the Creator of all things. From the vast and seemingly endless universe to the microscopic world of organisms the naked eye cannot see, He never ceases to amaze us with the way He created this world.

Likewise, when we look around ourselves, we can see how humans have changed the face of this planet by operating in the same creative spirit God has designed us with.

Many times for better, sometimes for worse, mankind has made amazing contributions while exercising dominion over the Earth. Just think of the breathtaking majesty of the pyramids or the huge skyscrapers that decorate the skyline of every major city around the world!

Rocket science, art and life-giving advances in the medical field form an array of how humanity has developed and is still displaying the marvelous gifts God gave us.

Each and every one of these was approached with a godly, entrepreneurial spirit.

Although modern day education tends to stifle it, this creativity is so much part of us that it will always rise up from within and result in some kind of big or small contribution to this world.

You, dear woman entrepreneur, are not an exception. Resourcefulness is part of your nature and you could not get rid of it even if you wanted to. If you don't feel very smart or creative right now and don't seem to have lots of new ideas, it's probably because you've been trained to shut down that important part of your being.

Then it's time for you to awaken to your God-given entrepreneurial gifting!

Why Do People Struggle With Having Extraordinary Ideas?

If you feel you have lost your entrepreneurial spirit and your creativity, then it's time to become aware of the way you have been trained to think.

Traditional education tends to create apathy in human beings. Just think about this: The typical classroom setting with a frontal teaching approach cannot survive with 30 students who freely manifest their entrepreneurial spirit.

Any duckling who dances out of the row is nudged back into it in many different ways, even to the extreme of using medications.

In one of our children's schools almost 25% of the students were diagnosed with Attention Deficit Disorder in the fourth grade! Really? If the system is manifesting these kinds of problems, maybe there is something wrong with the system!

John Taylor Gatto, a New York Teacher of the Year award winner and author of several revolutionary books about education, made the following interesting observation:

"A few years back, the School of Government at Harvard issued advice to those planning a career in the global economy of the future; it said that school credentials would be devalued compared to real world skills acquired by experience; it identified 10 qualities to acquire to meet the changing standards, none of which are usually found stressed by public schooling:

"1. Ability to define problems without a guide.

"2. Ability to ask questions that challenge common assumptions.

"3. Ability to work without guidance.

"4. Ability to work absolutely alone.

"5. Ability to persuade others that yours is the right course.

"6. Ability to debate issues and techniques in public.

"7. Ability to re-organize information into new patterns.

"8. Ability to discard irrelevant information.

"9. Ability to think dialectically.

"10. Ability to think inductively, deductively, and heuristically."

Do you think a school could function if children were encouraged to challenge prevailing assumptions? I don't think so! It has been designed to be a system that produces a perfect employee: somebody who is capable of blindly following the rules of another person's agenda.

What does that mean for today's entrepreneurs?

As an enterprising risk taker who seizes the initiative you have to realize that your environment is crucial. Most people you are surrounded with, probably even those in your closest circle, passed through the same system and don't even question their lack of curiosity and resourcefulness.

That is why it is so important to surround yourself with entrepreneurial people who think differently and can become role models that understand your vision and inspire you to boost your creativity and embrace the possibility of turning your ideas into good business opportunities.

Basically, there are three ways you can approach this change in your life:

1. The easiest way to enter into immediate personal contact with great thinkers is through their books. Determine to read books and biographies by and about famous entrepreneurs and businesspeople you admire.

2. Another way to become comfortable with the entrepreneurial mindset is through involvement with networking opportunities like conferences, events and even small gatherings, such as *Meetup.com* groups, in your town. By socializing with like-minded people, you will find a place where you can feel understood and encouraged in your endeavor to create a business.

3. In my experience, the third option is the best and most life-transforming: invest in a good mentor. In all of my studies about education during our homeschooling experience, I found

that the most effective way to learn is by being "discipled" by an expert.

Jesus used that modality to teach his disciples. He lived with them, walked with them and cultivated a personal contact with each apostle. That way He modelled for them how to go about the ministry. Later, in *The Book of Acts*, one can read how they changed their world by replicating what He taught them.

In a similar way having close contact with somebody who can see your business through the lens of a big thinker will rapidly lead you to a new level of growth, as a person and as an entrepreneur. Even though it is a big investment, in the long run this will save you money, time and a lot of headaches!

It is the best way to get rid of the mental chains that are holding you back from manifesting your true potential as a businesswoman.

Renewing Your Mind: Your Own Mental Chains

One of the biggest struggles I had as a businesswoman was—believe it or not—with my Christian faith. Or, let's say, what I believed my Christian path should look like. I felt bad about wanting to open a business and not dedicating all my energies to a nobler cause. I felt guilty about pouring so much of my energy and time into a business venture, when I really thought I should be focusing on producing lasting and eternal fruit by changing people's lives through the Gospel.

I yearned to stay at the place I called "the spiritual transaction versus the money transaction": giving freely of my time and effort to impact other's lives versus charging money to bring forth a change in them.

Little did I know that this belief was fueled by fear—not by faith. Deep down inside, I was afraid of losing the acceptance of God and of people by choosing the money transaction above the spiritual one.

This fear-based belief affected everything in my business. The niche I chose, my energy to move forward with new projects, the amount I charged, the way I charged, etc.

I can also observe this in many of my clients. They are beautiful, smart, capable and very compassionate women who love to help people transform their lives. Yet they have a deep struggle when it comes to making money with their gifts.

- They give away a lot for free.
- They undercharge.
- They over deliver.
- They serve a niche that does not value them.
- They have trouble closing sales.
- They don't have healthy boundaries with their clients.
- People don't pay them on time.

And the list goes on and on.

You can see how one wrong belief can stifle your growth in business tremendously!

It is pretty dangerous when that belief comes from a place you normally don't question: your church. If you are a God loving Christian, you are committed to going to church. That's just what a Christian does, right?

Let me be very honest with you and say things that need to be said: I love the church of God, the believers. I have received life-changing discipleship from many of them and I am eternally thankful for these selfless people who poured their very life into me.

But I have come to abhor the church culture that is prevalent in many places of worship nowadays. After a very painful and profound search for Truth, I realized that the root of my problem with my business is the prevalent church culture I was deeply involved in back then.

I know it may come as a shock to you, but many messages that are preached from the pulpit originate from manmade traditions and laws that have been widely accepted and have very little to do with God Himself.

At their best they are Bible-based messages that give you wisdom and healthy guidelines to live your life by. At their worst they are legalistic and demanding, leaving you full of condemnation and with feelings of unworthiness.

If you think about it, this is nothing new in the history of mankind. We seem to automatically, by default, drift towards a legalistic approach in our relationship to God. It circumvents a lot of effort to develop our spirituality and makes us feel good about ourselves when we manage to somehow reach the high standards that religion puts on people.

Historically, every new movement that bought a fresh revelation from God to mankind was persecuted by the church, not by the rest of the world. Jesus Himself was plotted against by the churchy guys.

That is why it is so important that you are aware of that Pharisee that dwells in each one of us, that small, legalistic voice that loves to point out everything we do wrong in our lives.

The sad thing is that this voice is strengthened—and not weakened—by the messages preached every Sunday in many churches.

I am in no way suggesting you leave your church, but urge you to spend your own time in God's Word, so you can recognize and filter out anything that is not from God Himself when you listen to a well-meaning preacher who is also human and therefore prone to making mistakes.

Just ask yourself: are you hearing the Gospel, the good news of how Jesus died for you, so you could be righteous before God, receive his unconditional grace, love and mercy and live the *zoe* life, the very life of God?

Or do you get a list of what you have to do and what you have to stop doing, in order to be a "good" Christian?

Whenever you feel condemned by a message, I can assure you, that was not from God.

Jesus said in *John* 3:17 New King James Version:

"For God did not send His Son into the world to condemn the world, but that the world through Him might be saved."

If you feel you are not worthy of God's love or that you will never be able to live up to His standards, then you are sitting in a prison cell, even though Jesus already came to set you free more than 2000 years ago!

In God's eyes, you are worthy and His perfect standards have been met, through the finished work of Jesus, on the cross. That is what His unconditional love is all about: He loves you, with no strings attached!

The only way to break free and get detoxed from religion is by learning what the True Gospel is all about. It will renew your mind about much more than money and wealth and you will prosper in all areas of your life, according to God's grand design.

3 *John* 1:2 New King James Version states:

"Beloved, I pray that you may prosper in all things and be in health, just as your soul prospers."

I did not want to defraud God by dedicating so much of my time to my business, and suffered a lot in this area. If you identify with my struggles, I want to dig deeper. Been there, done that. I can help you in this area!

Will the True Gospel Please Stand Up?

It will surprise you to find that the Gospel, the central message of what Jesus taught and commended us to preach to the world, is seldom taught in church, except for evangelistic endeavors to convert unbelievers.

During these events delivered on a one to one basis or even to huge crowds, it is taught that God sent His son Jesus to die for us, as a required sacrifice for our sins, so that we could come to a right standing with God again and enter into a profound and beautiful personal relationship with Him, just like He has always intended for us:

John 3:16 New King James Version: "For God so loved the world that He gave His only begotten Son, that whoever believes in Him should not perish but have everlasting life."

The Bible clearly states that this is a gift from God. There is nothing required from you to receive it. It is given by grace, an unmerited favor God lavishly and mercifully poured upon us, because of His unconditional love for us.

According to *Ephesians* 2:10 New King James Version:

"For we are His workmanship, created in Christ Jesus for good works, which God prepared beforehand that we should walk in them."

It is a beautiful message that changed my life back in 1993, when I gave my life to Jesus. Just the concept of realizing that God loved me in spite of all my "stuff," that He was not holding anything against me, but, on the contrary, waiting with His arms open wide so I could enter into an intimate and life-changing relationship with Him, impacted my life powerfully.

Love has that power. It can dramatically change a human being, more than any other force ever created, and God is love. I have seen this same love heal people, liberate them from lethal addictions, heal their relationships and completely turn their lives around.

I have also seen how this change does not last long for many of them. In church circles it is called "your first love" and you are warned about losing it.

The reason for this possible loss of your experiencing God's love for the first time is that your spirit is born again when you convert to Christianity, but your mind and body are not. They still want to keep on living according to your former habits and patterns of thought.

It is crucial for new Christians to be willing to transform their mind, so they can fully benefit from everything Jesus died for them to have.

Romans 12:2 New King James Version asserts: "And do not be conformed to this world, but be transformed by the renewing of your mind, that you may prove what is that good and acceptable and perfect will of God."

In other words, you can be a Christian, but still not fully benefit from your position as a child of God out of sheer ignorance. Here is a story that will help you understand what I mean:

I have been travelling quite a lot lately and had not realized that I had upgraded to Priority standard and could use this wonderful convenience of boarding the planes I flew in by using the preference line, without going through the long queue.

The bad thing is that almost a year passed until I noticed it! I would stand in the long queue, looking at how the passengers in the preferred line were able to board the plane first and wondering what it would feel like to have that privilege and what I'd have to do to become one of these passengers receiving preferential treatment.

The same thing happens to many Christians. They convert to Christianity, but then they never find out what the amazing promises are that God has for them and they end up living at much lower levels than those that God intended them to have.

2 *Peter* 1:2–4 New King James Version states:

"Grace and peace be multiplied to you in the knowledge of God and of Jesus our Lord, as His divine power has given to us all things that pertain to life and godliness, through the knowledge of Him who called us by glory and virtue, by which have been given to us exceedingly great and precious promises, that through these you may be partakers of the divine nature, having escaped the corruption that is in the world through lust."

Ironically, this lack of mind transformation is reinforced by today's church culture. The sinner who was saved by grace the day before and is now hungry to learn more from God is suddenly confronted with the duty-driven Christianity that is professed in the church culture.

God is presented as a demanding person who will only bless you if you read your Bible, go to church regularly and obediently serve Him. Oh, and did I forget to mention the Ten Commandments? Of course, you have to comply with them, too!

In other words, you have to be perfect.

That is why many churches are not successful in changing people's lives and are always half empty, because nobody is attracted by a message that constantly finds you faulty and not good enough.

Many people lose their first fascination with their new life in Christ and settle for the church version of Christianity that will perpetually keep them in a place of condemnation and rob them of the abundant life Jesus died for them to have.

What should really happen is that the same message of God's grace, love and mercy should keep on flowing into the believer's life to gradually heal spiritual, physical and emotional wounds and reveal to them what God has made available for them: the *Zoe* life, a life full of joy, peace and fulfillment that was given by grace.

Believe and You Shall Receive

Once this powerful process starts, your mind becomes mentally aligned with God's Word and this new, godly life starts manifesting in every area of your life. That is the way God designed our brain to function: to receive His Truth and become a spiritual womb that powerfully manifests what it is yearning for.

The power of this mind transformation is even evident outside the church. Many books like *The Secret* and *The Law of Attraction* talk about how your mind can powerfully manifest what it desires.

Surprisingly, non-Christians are operating in this principle better than the very people who profess to know God the best.

In his famous book, *Think and Grow Rich*, Napoleon Hill teaches about this power and states that he has seen it operate in very few Christians and mentions his surprise as to why most Christians don't have a clue about it.

Christians have come to rebuke this power as being heretical, because it has not been taught in centuries and they are ignorant of it. They don't know that it comes from God Himself and was given to us so we could be good stewards of this world, through His power in us and according to His design and plan.

Of course, this power can be used in a godly way or in an ungodly way. That is the freedom God has given us and that mankind abused by eating the fruit from the tree of good and evil in the Garden of Eden.

This is clearly shown when man resolved to build the Tower of Babel as high as the sky, and God had to disperse man, because he knew they could accomplish anything if they set their mind to it:

"But the Lord came down to see the city and the tower which the sons of men had built. And the Lord said, 'Indeed the people are one and they all have one language, and this is what they begin to do; now *nothing that they propose to do will be withheld from them.* Come, let Us go down and there confuse their language, that they may not understand one another's speech." (*Genesis* 11:1-9)

As you can see, overall, most churches fail to provide the answers to the real problems humanity faces, including the challenges of entrepreneurs. Due to church culture, Christians have compartmentalized their beliefs, so that their whole life is about church, the Bible and church activities. Anything else is considered to be "unspiritual," including spending time with unbelievers or "wasting" time on a hobby.

Jesus did not do that. On the contrary, his whole ministry took place outside of church and he was constantly surrounded by unbelievers. He sought to be among them, because He had a deep compassion for them. He spoke to them about the Kingdom of God, so He could show them how much God loved them and yearned to save them from their condition.

And that, my dear woman entrepreneur, is also your mission when you see yourself placed in the middle of the marketplace arena, asking yourself what on earth you are doing there!

You might not be able to openly preach to them, but you can be a witness to God in a place where most Christians don't dare to venture. You can be a light in that dark world, just by living out of your Christian faith as you do in all the other areas of your life.

Summary Chapter 3: The Spiritual Queen— The Entrepreneurial Woman in God's Eyes

- Most people see no connection between the messy, mundane marketplace and the purity and holiness of a spiritual life, although the Bible clearly shows how God Himself gives us the power to prosper in our lives.
- It is important to surround yourself with entrepreneurial people who think differently, because traditional education tends to suffocate our entrepreneurial spirit.

- Spend your own time in God's Word, so you can recognize and filter out condemning messages that are only manmade traditions and laws and have nothing to do with God Himself.
- In God's eyes, you are worthy and His perfect standards have been met, through the finished work of Jesus, on the cross. His love has the power to dramatically change your life.
- Christians often don't fully benefit from their position as children of God, because they ignore the amazing promises that God has for them.

Powerful Action Step:

Using the following scale, rate each of the situations I listed in this chapter according to how often you are engaging in each one.

1 = Never   2 = Sometimes   3 = Often   4 = Always

- You give away a lot for free.
- You don't charge what you know your service is worth.
- You tend to over deliver your time and your expertise with your clients.
- You serve a niche that does not value your work.
- You have trouble closing sales.
- You don't have clear boundaries with your family, your spouse, your vendors, your clients and your team.
- People don't pay you on time.

Choose the situations you rated a 3 or a 4 and answer the coaching question for Chapter 3 from my free workbook, "The Sleeping Queen's Workbook for Business Women", for each situation. (You can download it for free at www.TheQueensWorkbook.com)

—— *Chapter 4* ——
THE VICTORIOUS QUEEN
The Secret Battles of the Woman Entrepreneur

M aria Victoria struggled as she listened to the audio on her computer of her mastermind and group mentor for the third time. Everything he was teaching made so much sense:

- She had learned how to make an exhaustive research of her market niche;
- He had helped her to get clear about the different financing options available to her business;
- His teachings about marketing were priceless. Maria Victoria knew she had saved a lot of money by investing in paid publicity, using her business guru's unique marketing strategies.

Without a doubt, he was a great mentor!

But, as she tried to concentrate again on all the new information he was sharing in this training audio, writing down everything in her notebook, so she could review it afterwards, tears started to fill her eyes.

Deep inside of her something was missing, but she could not pinpoint exactly what it was.

What was wrong with her? She was doing everything she could to succeed in her business. She had invested in one of the best mentors she knew of and was implementing every new strategy he taught her. She had even experienced a slight growth in her revenue and her business was definitely changing.

Her drifting thoughts were jolted back to reality with loud laughter emanating from the audio she was listening to.

Of course, it was Pablo again! Pablo was a fellow student of her coaching group, a very charismatic and outgoing entrepreneur who was constantly reporting on the amazing growth he had experienced in his business over the last year.

Maria Victoria smiled. Everybody liked Pablo. He was such a happy-go-lucky guy. Business seemed to be a breeze for him. Whatever he put into practice in his business seemed to turn into money immediately. She could see how their mentor was pleased with him.

If only she could be a bit more like Pablo! He did not complicate things the way she did. His approach to business was so simple: learn, implement, grow. Then rinse and repeat. Of course he had challenges and he'd share those too, while mentioning that he felt like a warrior in a battle he was determined to win.

Maria Victoria's mind started to wander again. Why did running a business seem so much more complicated to her?

She tried to remember when was the last time she had run up against a wall in her business. Yes, she could relate to the analogy of it being like a war. She had faced many battles, but they were often very different to Pablo's.

There were those constant nagging questions that arose in her when she was planning her business and designing her services and products:

Would they meet the expectations of her clients? As hard as she tried, she never thought they were good enough, although she felt she was delivering much more than Pablo was—and at a lower price too!

Then there were those complicated clients. She did not know how not to give in to all their special requests.

There was also her family. She asked herself, did Pablo ever consider how his working overtime on his business affected his family?

It was certainly a huge issue for her!

She battled with her feelings of guilt towards her children every afternoon when they came home from school, and she was working on her business. In her former job as a teacher, she had been at home with them and had enjoyed paid vacations with them.

She also struggled with her parents' constant concern about her wellbeing. They were respectful, but it was obvious that they were not convinced she should pursue a new career as a businesswoman. They were always suggesting that she should get a good job, so she could live with a secure income and have more time for herself and for her children.

Her husband was supportive, but she noticed her long hours working at night were affecting their relationship too. Besides, she was refraining from sharing her excitement when she made money, because she sensed he'd question whether it was worthwhile to earn that amount after pouring so much time and effort into her business.

She even found herself asking similar questions. Why was she working so hard on this new project? It would be so much easier to go back to her old job. Her best friend was certainly happy there, especially after coming back from paid vacations to Hawaii.

Yet there was something about this business that gave her life a new dimension she'd never experienced before. For one thing, she knew it was an opportunity to change her and her family's lifestyle for the better.

But what really drove her onwards was the passion of sharing her knowledge and expertise with her clients and witnessing how this changed their lives.

Maria Victoria's countenance changed as she remembered her last client's testimonial about how his life had improved after working with her.

She felt a strong determination rise up in her. Yes, she was going to follow through with this project. For the sake of her future clients and her own sense of purpose and fulfillment, she was not going to give in to her doubt and confusions.

She turned up the volume of her computer, refocused on the voice of her mentor and started to take notes again.

The Evident Barriers

Just like Maria Victoria, many women struggle with their business in very different ways than men do, because a woman is wired differently than a man.

Most government programs and private mentoring programs are not as effective for women as they are for men, simply because they are designed for and conceived by men.

A man's approach to business is due to the warrior-like nature God created them with. It is analytical and logical, driven by their ego and natural tendency to movement, to display muscular energy, physical strength, will and control.

When designing a program for helping others in their businesses, they focus on:

- Aggressive goal setting;
- Numerical analyses and fact-based marketing strategies;
- Competitive positioning within their niche;
- Action based business strategies;
- Alpha Leadership skills.

What About Government Programs?

Governments worldwide are becoming more and more aware of the fact that female creativity and entrepreneurial potential are an underexploited source of economic growth and new jobs that should be developed. That's why new programs boosting feminine entrepreneurship are being offered with strong government support. These programs usually offer education on business building and marketing strategies, innovation, access to technology and special financing options.

Without a doubt these programs have helped many women build up their companies, but very often fail to address the hidden barriers that keep women from reaching their true potential as effective business owners.

What are Those Secret Battles Women Struggle With?

Maria Victoria´s doubts and confusion are very typical of the challenges many businesswomen encounter in their business daily and that are rarely addressed—or even understood—by male mentors.

A woman's approach to business reflects how God created women to approach all areas of their lives, so they could be a perfect complement to man in all of life's endeavors, not only in business.

Feminine power is associated with inner strength, softness, interior knowing, wisdom, intuition, creativity, nurturing, compassion and receptivity.

God's design is for man and woman to synergistically operate together, on a new and powerful level, with a highly effective combination of skills, capabilities and talents.

That is why a pure masculine approach to business—or any other area of life—can never lead to the full expression of what it is possible for humanity to achieve, in any endeavor, including in the business arena.

It will always overvalue the logical, analytical side of business and underutilize the soft, intuitive approach of the woman, producing a skewed result that does not reflect the true potential God has given mankind for achieving success and fulfilling entrepreneurship.

The truth is that the business world is still largely dominated by and taught from the masculine point of view for businesses, which is why most businesses led by women suffer from the lack of support for overcoming their own hidden challenges that keep them from developing a successful enterprise of their own.

I invite you to take a fresh look at my fictional woman entrepreneur, Maria Victoria, and her very real struggles with her own business:

You will see that a woman struggles much more with how her actions affect the people around her, especially her family. Her strong sense of solidarity with others will usually cause her to consider how her decisions will impact the lives of those that are dear to her.

That is why the aggressive masculine approach of "take action, no matter what" will not appeal to her. It will either paralyze her with fear of hurting others, or drive her to act—but then torment her because she does not feel as if she acted ethically with integrity.

Women need to approach business decisions with the permission to consider her family's needs too, as I elaborate on in the next Chapter: "The Businesswoman and Her Family: Either, or...or Both?"

Once she has the peace of mind from knowing that her business will not harm, but empower her loved ones, she'll be able to confidently move forward and unleash her full potential to attain impressive results in her business.

There is also another barrier women struggle with in business: their perfectionism.

Analysis Paralysis: How Do You Overcome Perfectionism?

Women tend to be much more perfectionist than their fellow male entrepreneurs. The direct result of this feminine trait is that they set much higher standards for themselves, are naturally less confident with their delivery, usually take longer to implement actions that further the growth of their company, due to their "analysis paralysis".

Whenever a woman isn't launching her products as fast as a man, selling her products and services at a lower price, or constantly fusses over how things can get done better, then she is most probably in her perfectionist mode.

This is especially deceptive, because at first glance perfectionism can appear to be a good thing. After all, what's wrong with trying to be as good as possible at what you do?

Most women are unaware of how they're trying to find their self-worth and get appreciation from others by being very hard on themselves with the high standards they set for themselves. They can easily feel tempted in finding their own value, even feelings of superiority, when they demand perfection from themselves.

This leads them to allow a very damaging spirit of control to rule their life that can lead them to become a slave to their unrealistically high standards.

That's why perfectionism can be one of the worst secret battles for the woman entrepreneur. It will cause her to delay implementation of new revenue streams, torment her with feelings of inadequacy and can drive her to burn out very fast in her business.

So, how do you overcome perfectionism?
Like all bad habits, it can be solved by consciously taking actions in the opposite direction:

1. **Less is more:**

A businesswoman can learn she does not always need to give all she has, nor does she need to deliver all that is necessary for the client at that moment. It is much better to fulfill clients' different needs through a wider diversity of offers, than smothering them by trying to fulfill all of their needs with one single sale.

2. **Learn to delegate to a perfectionist team:**

She has to understand that it's good to have high standards for her business, but that she is not the one who has to meet them all. This is where it's very important for her to learn to delegate and surround herself with people who are highly effective in their area of expertise.

Once she learns to trust others and their level of performance, she can let go of her exhausting need to pursue perfectionism through her own efforts.

3. **Get to the root of the problem:**

It is very important for her to get coaching on her need to get appreciation by being a perfectionist. Many times she is struggling with a lack of love—or lack of perceived love—from a primary caretaker and needs to recognize this and learn to forgive the person who caused this lack of self-worth in her.

No More Victim Mentality

It is relevant for a woman to become aware of these hidden barriers that are keeping her from experiencing success in her business. Far too often women blame their lack of success on circumstances, when in reality these inner barriers are holding them back from stepping fully into their identity as the successful businesswoman God intended them to be.

Yes, there is discrimination against us and yes, many times men have it easier in the business arena, but how much of that is because women have withdrawn into and succumbed to a victim mentality that has led them to simply accept the way things are?

Instead they could face their fears and doubts and boldly regain their position as a feminine leader who has a huge role to play—someone who can make an important contribution to the prosperity of her family and community.

Independent of your culture and the social circumstances of your surroundings you will always come up against odds when you stand up to claim your place of leadership. You must be prepared to battle against the resistance other people and/or groups of people will show when you raise your voice to take a stand for yourself and others.

This kind of opposition can be rough and even cruel, depending on the country you live in, but they are predictable and should be expected. You will most probably be able to identify with some forerunner of yours whose courage you can glean wisdom from; some heroine or hero who will inspire and motivate you to keep on going against the flow and questioning the status quo of your culture.

Throughout all of mankind's history changes in society have been initiated by people who dared to take a stand for what they believed was right.

If you're not happy with the opportunities you and other women entrepreneurs have in your country or society, see how you can wisely take a bold stand for what you believe in. People will respect you much more than you think, once you dare to speak out about a situation that's unfair. You'll be surprised to see how many who have kept silent will back you up when you dare to stand up and point out what, in your opinion, is wrong. That is what true leadership is all about!

Will it be easy? No. It's much easier to stay quiet and comply with what society is offering you right now.

This is where you will have to work on yourself from the inside out.

The Inside Job: How To Build Your Inner Strength

You must be prepared to confront inner negotiations with yourself about issues that will arise when you decide to grow as a leader and businesswoman.

Because these outward battles against your social circumstances are a walk in the park compared to the battles you will have within yourself. You'll have to be aware of—and more prepared—for these!

The inner battles go much deeper than the outward resistance you'll encounter from your culture, peers, family and loved ones. They will rage in your mind and ultimately determine whether you will remain a victim of your circumstances or a victor who overcomes them with courage.

The most debilitating questions will arise from within yourself, from the core of your spirit. These will directly affect your sense of identity and beliefs.

These, again, will affect every other aspect of your business:

- The decisions you'll make;
- The outcomes you'll pursue;
- The actions you'll take regarding your business;
- The actions you'll take vis-à-vis your surroundings.

If you want to stand up for what you truly believe in, you have to prepare yourself from the inside out. This is why your relationship with God is so important.

He will always point you back to your calling and to the vision He gave you for your business in the first place. Through the darkest hour, this will be your constant, like a huge rock in the middle of a raging sea.

It will be the place of peace and rest you will always be able to go back to when you need to reconnect with your "Big Why."

Dear entrepreneurial woman, your task may not always be an easy one. Of course it is much easier to stay in your comfort zone. That secure—but much too small—place where you feel you have everything under control. It will beckon you to come back into the place of being anonymous, where you can hide out, lick your wounds and return to victim mode.

It will draw you in with its tentacles when things get rough. But be aware that your true joy will not be found there. It is a place of nothing, comparable to being dead in life.

I encourage you to connect with the Most High God and draw from His grace and power instead. After all, it is He who called you to the business arena for a higher purpose and the battles are His, not yours!

The Courage of Setting Boundaries

As you fully embrace your calling as a businesswoman you'll want to move forward with clarity and purpose towards a clear outcome you want to achieve.

This automatically means you have to prioritize your time, money and all other resources, so that you can focus on reaching your goals and dreams.

This is where you encounter a new area of resistance, which you were not aware of when you had enough time and/or money to give to others: Setting clear boundaries with your family, your spouse, your vendors, your clients and your team.

For a woman this is not an easy task, because we are always aware of how our actions affect others. We want to serve everybody and make everybody happy. If that means sacrificing our own time and money, very often we don't think twice about doing it.

For a businesswoman this happens daily, in many different ways:

- If our husband asks us to do some errand when we really needed to write an article. Fine, we'll do that later.
- If our children need help with their homework when we need to call a client. Of course! They have always been the apple of your eye!
- If our clients extend their sessions with us, because they need to have that last question answered, sure! We are here to serve you, even when you need to go to the bathroom and you'll barely have time to do so before your next call.
- If a team member is not on time with the agreed upon schedule it's probably because, poor thing, they have so much work and it's okay if your project is postponed till tomorrow.

You can see that if you start tolerating these kind of situations in your life as a businesswoman your undertaking will suffer and you'll become frustrated—even resentful—against other people constantly violating your agenda.

The solution is not to chase them away once you're fed up with the situation, but to set healthy boundaries that'll benefit both sides. You can train people around you to become more responsible for themselves, instead of constantly draining your energy.

When you choose to not make yourself available at any given time, your message to the other person does not have to be: "I'm unavailable, so leave me alone, I'm doing my thing!"

It can perfectly well be: "I have chosen to take certain priorities in my daily schedule which I am responsible for, so that I can grow and move towards my goals. I know that you want the same for your life and I trust you have the power and wisdom to take responsibility and achieve that for yourself too."

The best way to do it with your family is by explaining to them how you feel and to point out where you need their understanding and support for your business. Then suggest some practical solutions to the issues that always come up and make you struggle between them and your business:

Set apart a block of time in the week when you will do errands for your home.

Tell your children that, at certain hours, mom cannot be interrupted unless the house burns down.

With your clients it's better to explain the way you work with them beforehand. You don't have to make this a set of rules you push on them, but clearly explain how they can also benefit from an organized and formal approach to their work with you.

Team members will also feel much better if you assume your role as a leader and point out sloppy attitudes. When you set high standards, they will comply with them. If you don't, they will not have anything to be accountable to.

Summary Chapter 4: The Victorious Queen— The Secret Battles of the Woman Entrepreneur

- The business world is still largely dominated by the masculine point of view for businesses, which is why many businesses led by women suffer from the lack of support for overcoming their own hidden challenges that keep them from developing a successful enterprise of their own.
- Once a woman has the peace of mind from knowing that her business will not harm, but empower her loved ones, she'll be able to confidently move forward and unleash her full potential to attain impressive results in her business.
- Women tend to be much more perfectionist than their fellow male entrepreneurs. They can easily feel tempted in finding their own value when they demand perfection from themselves.

- Your inner battles will rage in your mind and ultimately determine whether you will remain a victim of your circumstances or a victor who overcomes them with courage. This is why your relationship with God is so important.
- As you fully embrace your calling as a businesswoman you'll have to set healthy boundaries so you can to prioritize your time, money and all other resources.

Powerful Action Step:

Discover in what area you have been:

- Holding yourself back in your business out of fear it might affect a person you love?
- Delaying a project because of perfectionism?
- Neglecting to set a clear boundary with a family member, your spouse, clients, vendors or team members?

In what way has this affected your business?
What actions can you take to change this?
By when will you do this?

Chapter 5

THE QUEEN MOTHER

The Business Woman and Her Family:
Either, or...or Both?

My Story

I was sitting on my bed praying to God. There was a strong passion burning inside of me and I could not get rid of it.

We had been homeschooling our children for almost seven years, a profound experience that had turned out to be so much more than just another option to educate our four beloved children.

Up until this point, my husband, Robert, and I had come to question nearly everything we'd known and assumed to be correct about our educational system.

It had truly been a long quest for truth by searching for God's guidance to educate our children, a titanic task I did not feel prepared for. Nevertheless, Robert and I were determined to explore this option for our son, who had been in three different schools before even starting his first grade!

In our first year of homeschooling, I did all I knew to do, which was teaching them out of boring schoolbooks. As you can imagine, that did not last very long! Very soon I got burned out and was on my knees, articulating a very short, but effective prayer: "God, please help me!"

And He did. Little by little God gave me new revelations about education. As I started implementing what I learned, I immediately witnessed a huge change in our children.

Instead of my running after them to shove some required knowledge down their throats, they started pursuing their own projects and were motivated to search for the information they needed to complete their assignments on their own.

It was fascinating! My role had completely changed! From being a teacher who tried to get them interested in my agenda, I became a mentor who enjoyed observing them passionately pursue projects of their own choice.

You cannot imagine how much easier—and effective!—this option was. It's a good example of what God had shown me during my quest for a better educational option.

Matthew 11:28-30, New King James Version, states:

"Come to Me, all you who labor and are heavy laden, and I will give you rest. Take My yoke upon you and learn from Me, for I am gentle and lowly in heart, and you will find rest for your souls. For My yoke is easy and My burden is light."

This version of education was really a light burden for me. Even I got infected by that entrepreneurial spirit! During those years I rediscovered my childhood passion for writing and started on new book projects again.

After a few years of having a home that was buzzing with entrepreneurial activities, I was ready to share this marvelous experience with other parents! I knew of many parents who were struggling with the education of their children. It excited me to be able to show them that learning could be so different from what we had been taught it was.

What I really had on my heart was sharing, with young and old alike, the same message I am also sharing in this book: how God has a divine plan for each of our lives and has already provided everything we need to accomplish it.

I wanted to share how the teaching methods of the traditional school system violate the very essence of God's design for each and every human being: their distinct uniqueness, which can only flourish when given the freedom to develop according to an inner guidance by God Himself, rather than to an external "cookie-cutter style" agenda imposed by others, as if one size fits all.

But I did not know how to achieve that. Back in those days I was still homeschooling three of our four children and there was no way I could connect with other people on a consistent basis.

Yet I knew it was God who was nudging me into a new direction, because the passion for sharing this became stronger and stronger as time went by.

So I did what I always do when I don't know what to do: I prayed.

I still remember as if it were yesterday when the answer came. God gave me *Revelation* 3:8 New King James Version: "I know your works. See, I have set before you an open door, and no one can shut it; for you have a little strength, have kept My word, and have not denied My name."

Soon after that I felt a clear guidance to open an online business to reach people with this message throughout the whole world.

I started with my first web page in the year 2007 and the rest is history. Today I look back and am amazed at how I have developed as a businesswoman, in spite of all the obstacles I faced throughout these years.

The reason why it surprises me so much is because it took me very long to fully step into my God-assigned role of a businesswoman. I was always afraid it would damage my family.

Every hour I spent at my computer, working passionately on my new business, was later filled with feelings of guilt, because I felt I had neglected my children and my husband.

Then I tried to fix it by taking care of their needs—but felt bad again, because I had not spent enough time working on the business.

Very often I mentally postponed my business to some day in the future, when my children would not need me anymore. This often meant that I let profitable opportunities pass by, because I did not feel "ready" to fully embrace them. Or I was not very aggressive with my marketing, because I did not want to commit to a bigger volume of clients.

There was always this fear that one day I would pay the consequences for being this selfish person who was pursuing her own interests instead of committing to her family, as I should do.

So, my business was more of a hobby to me. I worked on it when I had some free time and found I could somehow compromise my commitment to it, minimizing my sense of guilt.

Thankfully, I could afford the luxury of not growing my business, because my husband had a good job. But, deep inside, I knew I was fooling myself by pretending I was somebody I did not dare to become.

Yet I just could not find the way to reconcile my business activities with my family life. I had a beautiful family and loved spending time with them, but I also wanted to grow my business. It was always this "either/or" struggle going on inside of me. In my mind, these areas were irreconcilable.

How Could They Possibly Fit In Together In My Life?
Many of my clients are mothers who have similar dilemmas pitting family against their business. As a matter of fact, countless women don't

even start their own business, even if they desire to do so, because they're afraid of how it will affect their families. Or they simply reject the idea, thinking they just don't have the time to do so. Just like me, they think that spending time away from their family, pursuing their business, could cause damage.

Back then I did not realize that this was a misconception about my role as a mother and a wife. From the time they are little children females are trained to serve others, especially in Hispanic societies. If you add religious misconceptions about what it means to be a submissive wife, you have the perfect picture of the dear, unselfish woman who is always serving others, but dying inside of herself. She becomes a woman who often ends up feeling resentment and anger, because she has always deferred her own aspirations, postponing herself and her own interests in order to please others and live up to socially imposed expectations and unexamined assumptions about a woman's role.

Sadly enough, this approach to motherhood is encouraged by both men and women alike in many cultures, especially the Christian one. I have had brilliant clients who had good chances to open their own successful companies but put their projects on hold for months, because they felt they had to tend to home front matters instead.

At the end of this chapter I will refer to this point in more detail, because there are moments in a mother's life in which the demands from her family are particularly high, but I have found that my "either/or" approach is common to many women who could perfectly well run their business without neglecting their family duties.

How did I discover that?

It's actually very easy: I did what I should have done from the beginning. I took a close look at the virtuous woman, God's design for true womanhood.

Below are the verses I shared in greater detail in chapter 2 of this book that describe the virtuous woman's entrepreneurial spirit, her money managing skills and industriousness.

The Virtuous Woman and Her Husband

There are two verses in the Bible referring specifically to her relationship with her husband and to how she affects her husband's life. According to the New King James Version of *The Book of Proverbs 31: 23*:

> "Her husband is known in the gates,
> When he sits among the elders of the land."

It's often said that behind every great man you'll find a great woman. The admirable traits of a good wife can secure respect for her husband as well. The city gates are where much of ancient commerce was conducted. So it is not unreasonable to conclude that the husband was conducting his own business affairs there.

It is interesting to note how the virtuous wife managed to back him up so well in his business dealings, while managing her own endeavors at the same time as well. Was she some kind of a super-duper efficient and organized lady who somehow managed to run her business(es) and then rush home to support her husband, so he could be successful as well?

I don't think so. Again, I don't believe God sets unrealistic standards for people to attain. It is we who make everything so complicated. Like myself, with my "either/or" approach to doing business.

I personally believe the virtuous woman supported her husband by having her business and fully stepping into her own potential on her own initiative. Not with the fear of risking a happy marriage, but, on the contrary, with the assurance that it would benefit him.

We can easily see that she was a true blessing to her husband in *Proverbs* 31, Verse 11:

"The heart of her husband safely trusts her;
So he will have no lack of gain."

What if she could be such a blessing to him because she was savvy in business and money management and not in spite of it?

The same question goes for her children, who are mentioned in Verse 28 together with the husband:

"Her children rise up and call her blessed;
Her husband also, and he praises her:"

Yikes! This family really seemed to be extremely happy with this industrious, busy and accomplished businesswoman.

Have we missed something? Is it possible that maybe, just maybe, the sweet, submissive and domestic role society has assigned for women falls short of everything God intended us to be as mothers, wives, daughters and feminine leaders in our communities?

Ladies, there is something clearly wrong with our perception of the woman being at home, only taking care of the children and domestic affairs, while the man goes out to hunt in the wilderness and provide for them. Again, there is a moment when this might be necessary, when the children are small, but it should not go on forever!

The Submissive Woman: Hiding Out In Motherhood

I remember discussions I always had with my dear husband Robert, who has been very patient with my metamorphosis into businesswoman-ship and all the growing pains this entails.

Whenever a decision had to be made, I went into submissive wife mode and told him he had to decide, because he was the man of the house. Of course I had my own opinion and I would share it, but I was taught that when the rubber hits the road, the husband was the one who cuts the cake.

This would deeply frustrate him. Not because he was unable to make a decision on his own, but he badly wanted me to be part of it. What I was viewing as a lack of leadership on his part was really his need for me to step up as co-leader of the household and family we were running together.

He intuitively knew I was backing away from a responsibility that was truly mine. After all, both of us were co-founders of our family and household, so why should I not actively engage in running it alongside, instead of subordinated to, my soul mate? It makes so much sense when you consider God's description of marriage in *Genesis* 2:24:

> "Therefore a man shall leave his father and mother and be
> joined to his wife, and they shall become one flesh."

Once united, man and woman are not two separate human beings who run their lives on different levels, but they become a twosome that together, are so much more than one plus one! Both of their talents, abilities and experiences are joined together to complement each other and become a synergistic force that can achieve amazing things, much more than each of them could ever accomplish individually.

But that cannot happen if one of these power-twins withdraws into a passive, submissive role, in the name of self-denial and obedience, while the other one carries the greatest part of the load. That is actually a very comfortable place to hide out in!

Can it be that many well-meaning women, who enjoy being supported by their husbands while they look after their family, are actually affecting their loved one's negatively by thwarting their own process of personal development?

I know that it was comfortable for me to leave important matters like the family budget, money management and investments in my husband's hands. Little did I realize that I was also disempowering myself in these areas and that this was also affecting my daughters' approach to finances, as I was their role model.

Nowadays I am much more involved in our family finances and am better prepared to help my husband make important decisions concerning our financial future. But I had to let go of my limited idea of the mom role I was so tied to. It was a long and painful growth process, mainly because I had to invent the way to reconcile my mother role with my part as a businesswoman on my own.

It's my ardent wish that this book may be a helpful companion on your own evolution from "mom to businesswoman." Although the circumstances from one family to the other vary a lot, I do believe women who desire to have their own businesses can legitimately ask themselves if they are really so badly needed at home as they think they are.

A Word About Mothering Versus Smothering Your Children

Many well-meaning mothers are so used to being there for their families to solve all their problems that they stifle their children's growth by not allowing them to take responsibility for their lives and solving many of their own problems.

Some women even go so far that they find their purpose in life is serving their family the best they can. Needless to say how this can be very damaging for their children. They will learn very fast what they can easily dump on their mother so they don't have to get things done on their own.

By not requiring her children to take responsibility for their lives she's training them to become lazy, immature adults who will easily succumb when faced with difficult circumstances.

You'll be surprised how much a child can help at home, even at a very young age. They can set the table, wash the dishes, fold the laundry, sweep the floor and much more.

By letting go of what you regard as your responsibility and providing a healthy space for them to develop their own independence, you will have more time and energy for your business and they will learn to solve their own problems, without having to rely on you for everything.

How Your Personal Development
Affects Every Person Around You

What spurred me forward in my decision to be more resolute in carving out the time to fully commit to my business was the realization that this decision would not have a negative, but a positive effect on my children.

Again, it was the virtuous woman who clearly served as a powerful example of a woman who lived her life to its fullest while positively impacting the people around her, including her children.

I tried to picture myself as her daughter, and I must say, the idea appealed to me! First of all, her daughters had an awesome role model to follow. Their mother was not only kind, generous, wise and loving, she was also rich. As a full-fledged business woman who had a knack for investing money and a great sense for beauty, she must have taught her daughters a thing or two about successful entrepreneurship and the personal fulfillment that comes with it!

Seen from a daughter's perspective, it dawned on me that the virtuous woman did not have the either/or dilemma so many women struggle with today. She just did life in one piece, beautifully integrating and sharing her own personal achievements with her family and loved ones.

Just like us, she only had 24 hours a day to accomplish this amazing feat, so there is no way she could have fulfilled both of these roles in a separate way. She did not compartmentalize herself by having a "family compartment" and "business compartment" in her life. They mingled with each other beautifully and fulfilled their purposes without one negatively affecting the other.

I can imagine the virtuous woman taking her children to the vineyard for a stroll, while at the same time watching over the harvesters, or taking a look at another property she wanted to buy.

Her daughters watched and learned as she designed the clothes she sold and witnessed how she negotiated with the resellers to get a good price for them. Afterwards they would visit a poor neighbor, to see how they could help out financially.

In this way the virtuous woman managed to run her business—and her life—well, without neglecting her offspring. On the contrary, her daily activities were the perfect platform for teaching them all she knew about life and entrepreneurship, in a very natural and effortless way.

In our era we might not have businesses that allow for our children to actively engage in and learn from us in a similar way as I describe above. But I can assure you that even if you don't take them along with you, they are watching and copying you! Children learn much more by modelling than by applying theoretical guidelines their parents give them to live their lives by.

I learned that very early on in parenthood. When the children were small and we wanted to instill good reading habits in them, we could tell them to read as much as we wanted to, but they only picked up their books when they saw us doing it.

If you want your children to be entrepreneurial, to love learning, to engage in a self-directed personal growth process and to not conform to the lower standards of their average peers, then you need to do that too.

Just think of the potential this has for them! If they witness you daring to step up into a leadership role and give voice to a message you passionately want to share with others, they will feel inspired to do the same.

If you launch your own business to sell your expertise in the form of services or products that benefit others, while you receive the fulfillment and rewards that come with it, they will learn through firsthand experience how a woman can achieve personal growth and financial success with her own company.

In day-to-day life this may happen in a very natural way. The entrepreneurial mother can share the success of her latest launch at the lunch table. Or she can ask her daughters if they like the outfit she bought for her next speaking gig. She may even break down and cry as she shares the struggles she encounters with a client or team member.

In all of these situations she is sharing her life and modelling how to face it with an attitude of faith, strength and optimism.

That is exactly what will happen once you let go of your concerns for your family and decide to beautifully blend your mother role with your role as a businesswoman. It will be an amazing and life-changing journey for you, a priceless learning experience for your children and the rest of your circle of influence.

Summary Chapter 5: The Queen Mother—The Business Woman and Her Family: Either, or...or Both?

- Expectations from their society and religious misconceptions about what it means to be a submissive wife, have led mothers to believe that spending time away from their family, pursuing their business, could cause damage to her loved ones.
- The virtuous woman from *The Book of Proverbs* was a blessing to her family because she was savvy in business and money management and not in spite of it.
- Once united, man and woman are not two separate human beings who run their lives on different levels, but they become a twosome whose talents, abilities and experiences are joined together to complement each other and become a synergistic

force that can achieve amazing things, much more than each of them could ever accomplish individually.

- You can foster your children's maturity by providing a healthy space for them to develop their own independence. That way you will have more time and energy for your business and they will learn to solve their own problems, without having to rely on you for everything.

- If you want your children to be entrepreneurial, to love learning, to engage in a self-directed personal growth process and to not conform to the lower standards of their average peers, then you need to do that too.

Powerful Action Step:

Do you struggle with feelings of guilt because your business is interfering with your family life?

Based on the example of the virtuous woman, brainstorm different ways you can integrate both of your roles—that of the mother and of the business woman—so that you and your family can benefit from them.

Chapter 6

THE REIGNING QUEEN
Women in a Man's World

Marcela slammed the door and crawled into her bed. Tears of anger streamed down her face as she sobbed into her pillow. She felt helpless as she listened to her stepfather's raucous voice still thundering across the room downstairs. When was this ever going to stop?

After coming home half drunk, he had lashed out at her mother again. Thankfully her mother did not receive the blow, because she ducked behind the kitchen door and managed to jostle Marcela and her three younger sisters into another room upstairs.

But Marcela did not stay there. Although terrified, she was not going to let this man beat her mother up again. After making sure her sisters were safe she ran back downstairs. It was not as bad as other times. Too drunk to stand, he was sitting in the dining room, yelling at her mother at the top of his lungs.

Marcela quickly caught her mother's arm and begged her to come upstairs with them. But she refused to go. She even scolded her daughter and commanded her to leave her alone. Then Marcela's mother went into the kitchen to clean up the mess her stepfather had made, ignoring his incessant, roaring voice.

Marcela could not understand her mom. Why did she tolerate this treatment? How could she live with a man who constantly abused her physically? She did not deserve this! Her mother was a beautiful and hard working woman who had always tried to take good care of them after Marcela's father had abandoned them. But she always seemed to attract the wrong men. At first her relationship with Carlos, her stepfather, seemed to be a good choice. When they married they moved into a much better home and things seemed to go well. But now it had turned into a nightmare!

With horror she remembered the day when Carlos had even burst into their room and had started to attack her and her sisters. Her mother had managed to rescue them, but the next day she had acted as if nothing had happened.

That behavior puzzled her. She felt rage rising up inside of her, but this time it was against her mother. Why would a woman choose to silently put up with this degrading abuse? Not even the nicest home was worth living in with this kind of man!

A small, sobbing voice brought her back to reality. It was her youngest sister, Maria, standing beside her bed. Marcela took her into her arms and tucked her into the blankets beside her. As she gently stroked Maria's hair she swore to herself that she would never, ever let a man humiliate her like this! She would finish school, get a good education, work hard and earn a lot of money. She was going to be successful and no man was ever going be able to ruin her life!

After eight years Marcela was well on her way to achieving her goal. She had left home and was working hard as an accountant in a big company. Very soon her boss noticed she was a hard worker and had excellent leadership skills. So he promoted her to become the head of the department.

At first Marcela was delighted. Now she could move into that beautiful apartment next door and pay off her car! She was also aware of new possibilities opening up for her. She even wondered if she could soon get another promotion if she worked even harder? Better still, one day she wanted to run her very own accounting business!

But it wasn't that easy. Now that she had a higher position, she also faced new challenges. Marcela noticed a certain hostility coming from her fellow woman colleagues who were now under her. One of them had even accused her of being an ambitious villain.

With the men she had another problem. In her former position they had had a good relationship, some of them had even tried to date her, but now they did not seem to take her seriously. They even snickered behind her back after giving them their daily assignments. Then there was Marcos, her boss. She noticed how his eyes followed her when she walked through the office. She ignored him the best she could and tried to focus on her new job.

Marcela felt very lonely. She was starting to realize that this promotion had come with a price and that any future ones would, too. But nothing would deter her! She still remembered the night she swore to herself that she would be successful and would never let a man ruin her life!

Women and Their Vulnerability

It is important to understand how women are wired before referring to how they interact with men, even in the business arena.

God created women to be loving and supportive caretakers. They have a strong inner core that will help them endure the most difficult of circumstances, but a soft and very vulnerable heart when it comes to relationships. They tend to give themselves entirely to a man, while men often don't take relationships that seriously.

This makes women extremely vulnerable to being mistreated when manipulative men want to take advantage of them.

A woman will react to masculine manipulation in basically two ways, depending on many factors, including her culture, personality, education and financial situation:

She will either put up with it silently and even defend the man abusing her, like Marcela's mother did or she will refuse to open herself up to men and adopt a contentious position, like Marcela chose to do.

The Weaker Sex?

From a Biblical viewpoint, definitely not. God created man and woman as partners and assigned both of them with the task of being wise stewards of this planet, so they could reign over it together.

Jesus Himself, who claimed to do everything according to His Father's will, showed no difference in His treatment towards women. In a time when women were severely discriminated against, He surprised the society of His day by lovingly lifting female followers such as Mary Magdalene to positions of respect and dignity.

Women are definitely not the weaker sex, yet they are very often misrepresented in that way. Even after all the advancements of equality and social justice in our modern society, we are being constantly bombarded with messages that present the woman with an image that emphasizes physical attractiveness over her intellectual abilities and thus undermines any development of entrepreneurial or leadership skills a woman might choose to pursue.

The Power of the Media

The power of the media has caused a lot of damage to women. It feeds gender stereotypes and does not represent the woman as a legitimate leader in modern society. According to a 2013 UNESCO report almost half of the news we watch daily perpetuates gender stereotypes.

In her eye-opening documentary *MissRepresentation* (see: www. MissRepresentation.org), Jennifer Siebel Newsom clearly shows how the media widens the gender gap instead of narrowing it on behalf of women.

The effects of the media on our perception of ourselves must not be underestimated. Teenagers are exposed to its influence an average of 10 hours a day through TV, movies, computers, mobile telephones and music.

According to Siebel Newsom, only 16% of media is directed by women. This fact explains why women are easily misrepresented in the media overall. Very often men will project a distorted image of a woman, using the female body as an excellent object for boosting sales on virtually anything. The subliminal message directed to boys and girls alike is that the most important attribute of a woman are her looks, above any other innate ability.

From an early age on, little girls are bombarded with messages telling them their physical attractiveness is more important than any other asset they might possess, like being smart enough to stand out in a leadership position in the future. This leads to insecurity in young women, who tend to undervalue other skills and capabilities they might possess.

The other side of the coin is the image that movies project of women who do achieve and stand out as leaders. They are either presented as go-getter villains who dominate others through ambitious pursuits, or they adopt the ultra-feminist version of the power woman who is clearly smarter and more capable than men.

Let's take a look at both of these fictional images we are sold on daily by the media:

The Villain Woman

She is ruthless, selfish, domineering and cruel. Once she gains the power to show her true self, the villain woman is pictured as a despicable monster lording it over everybody else.

The message behind this trope is a silent reprimand to little girls and women alike: "This is what you will look like if you unleash your ambition." The ambitious villain woman caricature is probably responsible for holding many women back from fully stepping into their feminine leadership role.

I know how deep this message can penetrate, as I also feared becoming like her and losing the acceptance of my loved ones if I dared to step out of my silent and submissive mode. My anxiety was very real to me: If I pursued my own desire for personal development it would automatically take away time, effort and energy invested in the people around me. So I reasoned that ambitious business women must become selfish and bossy to get the job done.

But do they really? Is ambition even a bad thing to have?

What exactly is ambition and is it good or bad?

If you are an entrepreneurial woman, it is highly probable that:

- You are constantly pursuing goals that challenge you to grow more.
- You want to increase your income at all times.
- You want to stand out as the best option in your niche market.

All of these qualities can be listed under the word "ambition."

It is also highly probable you have received criticism for being like that, because ambition is not regarded as a positive quality in our society, especially when it comes from a woman.

That is not surprising, since the definition of ambition has a negative touch to it:

"An eager or strong desire to achieve something, such as fame or power."

Not every woman who builds a company wants to identify with that statement! Just by reading those words I can envision the classic feminine villain of the movies who would be able to sell her own mother just to quench her thirst for power and wealth.

Women are naturally compassionate with a strong sense of solidarity. That's why this concept of ambition triggers so much controversy among us. This makes women fear success, because we believe it will come at the cost of becoming a despicable person.

The villain woman has kept—and is still keeping—countless women from confidently stepping into the place of leadership God has assigned to them as entrepreneurs. They might feel comfortable with leading a charity or a non-profit organization, but a business? Opening their own company to make money causes them to heavily wrestle with feelings of guilt and fear.

If you are afraid of success because you fear becoming a bad person as a result of achieving it, I'll ask you a simple question: Are you a bad person now?

Because success will only magnify who you are right now.

A selfish person will inevitably magnify her bad character and manifest it in a bigger way once she has more power to do so.

On the other hand, if you are person who desires to be a positive agent of change in this world, then you will be able to do that in a much more powerful way once you have more financial resources and a wider level of influence in the world!

It all lies in understanding the true motivation for your ambition as a business woman.

So, the question is:

Is Ambition In a Woman Really a Bad Thing?

Ambition seems to be good at times, and at other times, it's not.

It is a complex topic that causes a lot of confusion in the life of a feminine entrepreneur. On one side, their inner ambition is driving them to go forward, but their fear of success is constantly holding them back.

As a mentor and coach to women entrepreneurs, I have seen that this confusion is expressed in many ways:

- Women charge much less than they could, because they assume their help should be for free.
- Women tend to have a bad relationship with money, because they believe it is wrong to pursue riches.
- They very often burn out, because they don't feel they are giving enough, so they over-deliver too much of their time and expertise.
- They get stuck, because they succumb to the constant push-me-pull-you of ambition versus fear of succeeding.
- They lose their focus and start getting dispersed, because they have not given themselves full permission to go forward with all their strength in their business.

If this describes you, then it's important to get clarity on the subject of ambition. It's crucial you confront the ambition that is driving you forward and the almost unconscious unwillingness to fully unleash it in your life and in your business.

The truth is that ambition in itself is neither good nor bad. What can harm you is the true motivation that is behind your ambition.

Our motivations are birthed in our hearts. They are the motor that ignite our actions, but they are not always evident, not even to ourselves. This results in actions that can be catalogued as ambitious and that can come from a good or a bad motivation. From the outside they look the same, but, from the inside, it's another story. And the results are diametrically opposite to each other.

How can you know if your motivation is good or bad for you?

Egocentrism Versus a Spirit of Service

Ambition can consume a person's life if it comes from a place of selfishness.

If everything you do in your business is only about you, then you are trying to measure yourself by your achievements. This will only set you up for frustration and delusion. You'll be impatient and unhappy, because you'll be intolerant of your mistakes.

If you are feeling like this now, please be honest with yourself. Maybe other people have laid expectations on you and are measuring you according to your achievements. Or maybe you have been conditioned to think you will only be loved more if you achieve more.

This happens to a lot of women who did not receive love or acceptance during their childhood. The best thing you can do is forgive the person who laid that burden on you, change your story and move forward in life. People love imperfectly because they have been loved imperfectly.

Healing comes by stepping fully into the unconditional and perfect love of God, your Creator. He does not measure you by your achievements. He loves you the way you are, even if you never achieve the ability to walk in your heartfelt mission. He will not be disappointed. There is actually nothing you can do to be more loved and accepted by Him. Just like a mother lovingly takes her baby into her arms without dreaming of how she can use her child someday, God's love for you has no strings attached. And it has no expiration date.

Yet there is nothing that will give you more joy than fulfilling the mission God has put in your heart. He has created you with a perfect plan for your life, so you can live it to the fullest and beyond your wildest dreams.

I love the concept of purposeful prosperity (the theme of my webpage at www.BettinaLangerfeldt.com) because it views a business as a mission that is not about you, but about something much bigger. It comes from a place of service and helpfulness to your clients and the certainty that you will be generously provided for by pursuing it.

A business can be an excellent venue to channel your talents and gifts to the world in a big way. By setting up business systems that allow you to reach a vast number of people for a long period of time, you can make a big difference in the lives of many with what you are passionate about.

This will not only bring financial success for you, but also a deep feeling of fulfillment that will surpass any level of happiness you might achieve by trying to please yourself only.

Dear entrepreneurial woman, put your eyes on the people who need your help. When your service comes from a place of compassion and love for your clients, channeled through a business that allows you to reach even more people in the future, you will truly prosper, feel fulfilled and satisfied.

Feminism, Redefined

Now that we have dealt with the topic of ambition, let's take a look at another misconception regarding gender stereotypes that is perpetuated by the media and has caused just as much harm to the woman entrepreneur as the villain typecasting. Its origin is extreme feminism, which has resulted in the false image of a superwoman who is much smarter and capable than men are.

Thanks to the Feminist Movement that started in the Western world in the late 19th century, countless advantages have been achieved on behalf of women. There is no doubt that since then, the conditions of women in the areas of reproductive rights, domestic violence, maternity leave, equal pay, women's suffrage, sexual harassment and sexual violence have improved.

At first glance it has all been good for us. In the name of progress, women have finally opened doors previously closed for centuries.

But has it really ALL been good?

Feminism has elevated the woman to be the equal of a man, which naturally leads to a competing against—instead of complimenting—each other. What initially came with the intention of raising the woman's circumstances in Western society has sorely backfired on her!

Radical feminists have taken the pendulum way to the other side of the spectrum. Although feminism began with noble goals, it has degraded into a dangerous and negative mindset that has resulted in a direct assault against the woman herself. Just like any other cause that strives for equality, the feminist movement has done a lot of harm to women by going too far into unhealthy extremes.

It scorns womanhood by implying that a woman must become like a man in order to be equal to him, because, as a woman, she's not good enough. By misunderstanding their true role, feminist women have caused the breakdown of the very things they were fighting for in the first place: herself and her family.

Let's take a look at what happens when the woman competes with and takes the place of the man.

She's the Boss!
As a female entrepreneur you are probably already aware of the potential power God has given you and it is very important for you to understand how to handle it wisely.

Empowered women are on the rise. Movies are made about women who are smarter and more capable than men, books are written about heroines who have stood up against an unfaithful establishment run by men, and we can see women gaining more access to political, professional and corporate platforms that were unthinkable only 50 years ago.

Some pop culture examples are Veronica Sawyer, Xena, Lydia Deets, Coraline, Hermione Granger, Claire Huxtable, Veronica Mars, Wonder Woman, Harriet the Spy, Matilda, and, of course, Eowyn.

Let's take a look at what feminism's negative consequences are:

Men Are Missing In Action within the Family
The devaluation of men has had a negative effect on both women and men, as it undermines the leadership role a man assumes as a husband, father and citizen.

Let's be honest. Deep inside, each woman is still the fair princess who longs to be rescued from the dragon by her knight in shining armor. The problem is that the knights who would be eager to honor and fight for a woman in that manner have become an alarmingly endangered species! Sadly, in many cases, it's the ladies themselves who have undermined the leadership roles of men.

Why? Simple: Because in our complex, modern society many boys are raised by women or by men who were raised by women!

In the United States, 1 in 4 children under the age of 18—a total of about 17.4 million—are being raised without a father. (4 U.S. Census Bureau – Table C2. Household Relationship and Living Arrangements of Children Under 18 Years, by Age and Sex: 2014)

Young boys have been deprived of the role models they need in order to develop the necessary leadership skills for their adulthood as men. This has directly affected the woman herself, who is now often solely responsible for herself and her children.

In retrospect, what the woman has really achieved with her "emancipation," is that she has become more masculine by striving to be equal to man, instead of honing in on her natural feminine attributes to complement man in a powerful, yet graceful and feminine way.

The Important Contribution of Women to the Business World

It is becoming more and more apparent how the woman makes a vital contribution to the business world with her innate strengths, such as intuition, networking abilities and natural compassion and solidarism.

Even though the corporate world is still mainly a man's world, women have made inroads in this area slowly over time. Just 20 years ago, there were no female CEOs of Fortune 500 companies. Today, 26 women are serving as CEOs of Fortune 500 companies (5.2%). As of 2013, about one-in-six (16.9%) board members for Fortune 500 companies were women, up from 9.6% in 1995.(Catalyst: Women CEOs of the Fortune 1000; Catalyst: Women in the United States.)

According to Cherie Blair, founder of CB Foundation for Women, "There is no sustainable development unless we engage women. If we get this issue right, regardless of background, race or location, we will have a fairer, more prosperous and peaceful world."

Her statement is backed up by statistics: It is proven that women foment honesty in the workplace because, historically, it is much more difficult for a woman to be bribed or corrupted than it is for a man (Scherer, 2012).

This is even more evident in Hispanic culture: According to Ammje (Asociación Mexicana de Mujeres Empresarias Ammje, 2013), a woman will designate 70% of her income to her family, while men reportedly contribute only 30 to 40% of their resources to the family unit.

Women are also more faithful in paying off their debt when investing money in their business then men do. 99% of them pay off their debt entirely (Secretaría de Hacienda y Crédito Público, 2013).

It's evident that women play an important role as leaders in society, as they contribute with crucial talents and abilities that perfectly complement the more analytical approach men have to leadership. Both sexes were created to complement and never to compete with each other as leaders in society.

Once both genders are aware of their calling to collaborate, rather than to compete, a divine synergy takes place and their effectiveness for leadership is exponential, surpassing "one plus one equals two." It literally multiplies!

On the other hand, when women are not allowed to assume their role as co-leaders with men, society is robbed of their crucial contribution and thus the development of true prosperity and well-being for the whole community is jeopardized.

Yet there are still many instances in which men prefer not to work with women—and while I hate to admit this, it's often for legitimate reasons.

Don't Play the "Girl Card"

Last but not least, I'll end this chapter by touching upon a subject many women are not aware of when they pursue meaningful partnerships as co-leaders in a world ruled by men:

Beyond the maternity rights that women have quite successfully fought for in the past century, there are also justifiable reasons why some men don't like hiring women:

It's simply because women tend to be more complicated in the workplace. There are some cards women like to draw that disrupt the working environment:

- The "sexy" card with male colleagues.
- The "bitchy" card with female colleagues.
- The "bursting-out-in-tears" card with their superiors.

None of them have to be described in detail. We all know what we're talking about here.

The point is that if you, as a woman, want to make a contribution to the world by assuming positions of leadership, you will have to be willing to keep very high professional standards for yourself, so that you are taken seriously as a woman in a man's world.

Summary Chapter 6: The Reigning Queen—
Women in a Man's World

- Women are definitely not the weaker sex, yet they are very often misrepresented in that way, specially by the media, which feeds gender stereotypes and presents the woman with an image that emphasizes physical attractiveness over her intellectual abilities and thus undermines any development of entrepreneurial or leadership skills a woman might choose to pursue.

- The other side of the coin is the image that movies project of women who do achieve and stand out as leaders. They are either presented as go-getter villains who dominate others through ambitious pursuits, or they adopt the ultra-feminist version of the power woman who is clearly smarter and more capable than men.

- Ambition is a complex topic that may cause a lot of confusion in the life of a feminine entrepreneur. It is neither good nor bad. What can harm you is the true motivation that is behind your ambition.

- When your service comes from a place of compassion and love for your clients, channeled through a business that allows you to reach even more people in the future, you will truly prosper, feel fulfilled and satisfied.

- Women play an important role as leaders in society, as they contribute with crucial talents and abilities that perfectly complement the more analytical approach men have to leadership. Both sexes were created to complement and never to compete with each other as leaders in society.

Powerful Action Step:

What is a situation where you are holding back from leaping into a new opportunity, because you:

- Think a woman "should not do that".
- Feel you would disappoint somebody who has certain expectations of how you should live your life.
- Are afraid of being ambitious, because you believe that success in that area will affect you negatively.

Pick the option that is most true for you and complete the "Unleashing Your Courage" handout from my free workbook: "The Sleeping Queen's Workbook for Business Women" at www.TheQueensWorkbook.com

Chapter 7
THE CONFIDENT QUEEN
How to Own Your Value

E milia gulped. Her throat went dry and she had to cough. Thankfully she had a glass of water nearby and her client Monica could not see how nervous she was over the phone.

How much did she charge? Emilia looked at the number she had written down for what seemed to be the hundredth time. A whole month had passed by since she had outlined her fees for all of her products and services. If only she could be as confident about them now as she had felt back then!

These numbers seemed to jump off the page, accusing her of charging too much. She reflected on Monica's difficult situation and how badly she needed her help. Deep compassion filled her as Emilia remembered how Monica had broken down when she shared from her heart what she was going through.

Monica was on the verge of burning out due to excessive work. She badly desired a promotion, but felt her boss did not see her as capable of taking on a new level of responsibility and leadership.

Emilia knew she could help her get on her feet again! While Monica was sharing her daily challenges at work, Emilia had already outlined the exact steps she would take her through to help Monica rise to the top of her profession. She'd already helped other women executives successfully achieve promotions at their workplaces.

Emilia smiled, realizing she had a knack at pinpointing problems that were holding her clients back and helping them regain their confidence, empowering them to step fully into their true potential in the companies they worked for.

Emilia also knew her coaching services changed her clients' lives and was eager to help Monica gain the respect of her superiors and be able to prove to them what she was capable of doing for them.

While Emilia's mind was filled with these thoughts, Monica started a long explanation of her financial situation. To make matters worse, Monica was in debt and needed a raise to be able to pay off the sum she owed. Her husband had lost his job and they were relying on her sole income.

"What a mess!" Emilia mused while listening to Monica's story. In her mind, the possibility of working with Monica dwindled away. She was not going to have the amount of money to pay her!

Then an idea struck Emilia: What if she offered to work half price for Monica? Then she would surely be able to pay her! But then Emilia remembered she'd already done that before but then felt resentful afterwards, because that client didn't even thank her for lowering her fees and even demanded lots of extra time during their coaching sessions.

No, she was not going to do that again! But she could give Monica a discount. That sounded like a good idea!

All these thoughts flashed through Emilia's mind as she realized Monica had stopped talking on the phone.

Monica wanted to know: How much does it cost to work with you?

Emilia quickly glanced at the number again, made a mental discount and told Monica she had a special offer she'd specifically designed to help her and disclosed the number.

Then the dreaded silence came. Monica was not answering! Maybe she didn't have the money to pay her, even with the discount? But she wanted to work with her so badly!

Emilia blurted out: "I can also offer you a payment plan, if you prefer that!"

Monica's voice finally came on the phone again: "Oh yes. How much was that?"

Emilia quickly reached for her calculator and set up a payment plan for the discounted price. In her excitement at the possibility of getting hired, she totally forgot to charge an additional fee for the payment plan and simply divided the discounted amount by the number of months they would be working together.

When Emilia saw the amount of each payment, her heart sank. It was much less than she wanted to earn. But it was already too late; she had stated what her price was. Monica said she wanted to work with her and they hung up.

Emilia was thrilled to have a new client, but also felt disempowered, as she glared at the actual number she had really wanted to charge for her services.

She had done it again! She had charged much less than she had really intended to! Although Emilia was going to enjoy working with Monica, she was still stuck with the same price she had charged for the last three years!

She took a last glance at the number and resolved to charge that amount the next time a client wanted to work with her. But then again, would she dare to do it?

She folded the piece of paper and tucked it into her drawer. One day, when she had more experience and was a well-known coach, she would certainly be confident enough to charge that fee! But until then it seemed as if the coach needed a coach.

For now Emilia would enjoy helping Monica to stop sabotaging herself in her current position so she could be taken seriously by her superiors and get the promotion she yearned for.

Why Women Undercharge

Chronic undercharging is rampant in the female business world, especially among service-based firms. Women often leave college with higher degrees than men, but are already earning 10 percent less than their male colleagues when they are 30 years old.

There are several causes for this. The most obvious ones are external circumstances, like the discrimination women are still victimized by to a greater or lesser degree, depending on their cultural background.

But there are also inner barriers that hold women back from charging more for their services. These inner barricades are much more powerful obstacles to overcome, since most businesswomen are not even aware of them.

The fear of losing clients and lack of self-esteem are only symptoms of a much deeper misconception—or, to be more precise, lack of education—women have about service, money and marketing.

Created To Serve

Emilia's profound desire to help her client, even at a lower price that might not even pay for the cost of her services, is a classic example of the way most women reason when they charge lower fees.

Emilia's mindset mirrors one of the main reasons why many women don't charge enough: at the core of their being they are all about helping others. The compassionate and caring female heart will tend to overlook any obstacle that stands between a woman and the possibility to make a difference in another person's life, including her fees. This approach can even lead to giving their expertise away for free.

God created us as nurturers and supporters to the people around us and to experience true joy when we give to others. Deep in our hearts, we're passionate about impacting other people's lives.

That's why women go into the extreme "money-does-not-matter mode," because we experience true happiness and a profound sense of fulfillment when we can make a difference by helping others.

Don't Mix Your Charity With Your Business!

But this is a shortsighted approach to leaving a legacy with your talents and expertise. Just because money is not the main reason why you chose your profession, this doesn't mean you can ignore it and still expect to thrive!

You need to create a solid financial structure that allows you not only to stay in business, but to also prosper financially so you will be able to help people as much as you want, without jeopardizing your future as a successful businesswoman who impacts her community with her talents and expertise.

Let's face facts: even charitable organizations and ministries have to be savvy about how they finance their entities! I learned this the hard way, with an exceptional ministry that supported me through our first homeschooling years:

Back then I felt very lonely, because, in my home country (Chile), homeschooling was unheard of and there were very few people who took their children out of school to raise them at home. We were also facing much criticism from peers and family, which, combined with our own insecurities about how to go about giving our children a quality education, made us yearn to share with likeminded parents who would understand our vision and support us.

Luckily we had the Internet, so I spent lots of time researching homeschooling and very soon found a woman whose Bible-based, educational philosophy impacted me profoundly, because it was very different from anything I had ever heard of before.

She had a wonderful website with an interactive forum that turned out to be my "haven" where I could take refuge and find companionship with other homeschooling mothers.

I devoured every book she wrote, because her methods worked and completely changed our mindset about education. She turned out to be one of the main influencers of our new approach to education which led us to foster our children's leadership and entrepreneurial skills.

Looking back, she was God-sent to our family. Her teachings and encouragement supported me during those first homeschooling years. I dare say I would probably not have been able to persevere through those first years of uncertainty had it not been for this lady and her ministry. Furthermore, her teachings inspired me to discover and develop my own talents, a journey that eventually led me to open my first online business.

But the problem was that this amazing ministry that was impacting so many families suddenly closed its doors, practically overnight! They had run into financial problems. Her husband had to quit helping her and find a job, so she closed her website and the online forum simply disappeared.

As you can imagine, this sudden absence had a big impact on all of her followers, including our family. We found it to be inconceivable that such an important, life-changing message would no longer be heard. But I also learned an important lesson that I have never forgotten:

It does not matter how important and vital your services or products are—you will not be able to dedicate yourself to what you are passionate about if you don't educate yourself in how to finance your mission and make enough money to live well from it.

Since then I no longer hesitate when asked what I charge and state my fees with confidence, because I know this is the only way I can keep on impacting lives with my knowledge and expertise.

But undercharging is an even more complex issue. There are still other powerful reasons that cause women to undercharge. For example, offering your products and services to a wrong niche or using deficient marketing strategies will quickly lead to exhaustion and make a woman feel forced to lower her fees, even if she really does not have to.

Money is Not Important?

The other side of the same coin is not deeming money as important. Many women have a bad relationship with money, because they were taught to believe that money and the pursuit of it is a bad thing.

This tendency of seeing the pursuit of money as shamefully unspiritual has led many people who honestly want to make a good living to feel fear and shame around their prosperity and live a cynical lifestyle in which, on one hand, they devote huge amounts of their time and energy to creating wealth, but, at the same time, try to play down their achievements out of shame and guilt for possessing wealth.

This has also led many women to cultivate a bad relationship with money, because they choose to deny the importance that money has in their lives. They compartmentalize their personal finances from all the other areas of their life and are not aware of how money connects to their emotional, mental and physical stress that directly affects her family's wellbeing and even causes the vast majority of marriage problems and divorces.

True Prosperity

In the Bible it clearly states that wealth creation is not only spiritual, but highly desired by God for his people. He is the ultimate Entrepreneur, the Creator, and we are made in His image.

This is clearly seen in how Jews, God's people from the Old Testament, relate to money. Historically, the Jewish people have shown to be very good at not only handling, but also at multiplying money. The Jewish business genius is due to the fact that Judaism's spiritual regimen allows for a guilt-free appreciation of wealth accumulation.

In the Christian belief system, misconceptions about money and its evil power have their roots in religious beliefs originated in the poverty vows made by Catholic monks during medieval times. Since then money and everything that has to do with it is taught to be avoided in many Christian circles, leading to the prevalent negative manner in which people approach money in the Western hemisphere.

It is vitally important that the businesswoman understands that pursuing wealth through a business is not only spiritual; it is highly beneficial for the personal development of the woman, which will directly affect her family and her community.

How to Heal Your Relationship with Money
The most powerful way to get your money story straight is by going right back to where it started: your childhood. In coaching women about money, I have found that all of them have, in some way or other, made a silent agreement with themselves or with another person about how they view money, when they were very little.

This silent agreement is very often made to protect themselves from harm or to fill a deep need they feel in that moment. Later on, in their adult lives, this silent agreement does not serve them anymore, but it still governs their belief system and causes them to get stuck when they pursue financial growth.

One very good example is Valentina, one of my clients, whom I helped discover that her authoritative father made her believe, when she was little, that she would never be able to reach his standards. As an adult and brilliant coach, she kept on believing that she did not perform well enough as a coach, so she under charged her fees.

Once she made this connection and was led through a healing process of her past, she could quickly connect with her true worth and confidently charge a new level of fees that were unthinkable for her before.

After the root of this problem is taken care of there is still a vast field of practical money management that must be learned:

In my experience as a businesswoman, I have seen that many personal finance courses that are tailored by men are more difficult to implement by women. That is because women are much more susceptible to succumb to inner conflict around money. They need to eliminate emotional triggers such as guilt, shame or blame from their life before they can feel free to take aligned action in their personal and business finances.

Before they can change anything, they need to discover and acknowledge their unique money strengths and gifts, along with their money shadow-side that has always led them to repeat the same mistakes around money, over and over again.

In my opinion, one of the best approaches to experience a solid change in your money habits is that of Kendall Summerhawk's *Sacred Money Archetypes*. This unique evaluation considers the personality traits of each person and helps them design powerful money habits without violating the individuality of each woman.

I myself have successfully used my Archetypes to leverage my money strengths into a higher achievement level, without trying to fit into a box of "what I should do" with my money matters.

A Short Word About Your Niche and Your Marketing

This book covers the important subject of your niche and marketing in Chapters 9 and 10. For now I only want to mention that women often tend to charge less because they encounter difficulties in:

A) Their niche market: they are attracting and selling to the WRONG client.
B) Their marketing and selling strategy: they don't know how to attract new clients or sell their products or services once they do have an interested client.

If you were educated in the traditional school setting, like most of us, it's highly probable that you were not taught how to market yourself. Rest at peace, beloved entrepreneurial woman! All of this can be learned, just like you learned how to drive a car or ride your bicycle, when you were little.

I have also found that, more often than not, women entrepreneurs have trouble getting clients when they are not in the right market, or they have a much too broad marketing niche. This makes them constantly talk to prospective clients that either don't need—or don't value—their services enough. A third possibility is that they need and value their services, but don't have the money to pay for them.

All of these situations obviously reduce the success rate of their sales process and makes them prone to becoming chronic under chargers.

With this said, I want to reassure you: if you feel discouraged because of a low client enrollment level, don't take it personally. It's not because you or your services and products are not good enough. There is a lot you can do to reach an ideal client with the perfect solution and the right message, to get paid handsomely for what you do! As I said, I will talk more about marketing, sales and your niche later.

But the first thing that has to happen so you can raise your fees to a level that makes you dance for joy is that you connect with the true value you are delivering to your clients.

My Offer Is Not Too Expensive, It's Just that You Can't Afford It...
This can and should be your response when clients shy away from you once you name your price.

If you cannot fathom people hiring you for higher fees, then it's time you gain a deeper insight into the true value of what they are receiving through your services.

For example, in my case, I am a prosperity coach and business consultant for women entrepreneurs who are coaches, consultants or service-based business owners. I help them heal their relationship with money and implement business and marketing strategies that free up their time and help them create a thriving business doing what they are passionate about.

At a first glance, the transformation I offer is evident: a higher level of income, more and better clients, more free time and a higher level of professionalism.

That sounds wonderful, but, if I dig a bit deeper, I can find an amazing array of additional benefits that neither I nor my clients are aware of, unless I choose to bring them to light and charge accordingly:

Better Relationships
My clients tend to improve relationships with other people due to increased success in their business. Since most of my clients are women, they have a special concern for their children. Many learn to implement business systems that free up time they can then spend with their family, or become more available to their family by starting working from home.

Due to a better relationship and their empowerment with money, there is less tension around finances with spouses or partners. They also improve relationships with friends, colleagues and extended family, since they enjoy a higher level of self-confidence and personal fulfillment.

If you could label these benefits with a price, how much would that be? (Of course, certain things are priceless or, as *The Book of Proverbs* 31:10 says, you are: "A price above rubies.")

Their Health and Well-Being
By becoming unstuck in their business, they have a lower stress level, which automatically translates into better sleep, better eating habits and less anxiety. Additional time helps them dedicate themselves to a hobby or sports.

How much value is this benefit?

A Promising Future
Their future looks favorable and propitious. Businesswise they have a profitable and a scalable business model that will lead them to more expansion in the future. As they advance, new doors of opportunity open to an even broader level of influence with what they do. Moneywise they also have the tools and habits to retain more of what they earn. Their personal finances improve and they have less debt and/or more money laid up for their future.

How much is this worth?

Their Sense of Purpose and Fulfillment Soars
Since they are having a bigger impact with their business, they feel purposeful and significant.

What price does this have?

How much would the price of all these additional benefits be?

You are right, they are priceless!

What are the priceless ripple effects of your services and products?
Do you see how you can easily undervalue the transformation you deliver to clients?

I'd like to challenge you to brainstorm and make a list of at least 30 benefits your clients receive from investing in you, your products and services.

Leave that list in a place that is visible for you and read it every day, until you are absolutely convinced of the amazing value you are delivering. Once you are deeply connected to your true worth as a businesswoman you will not hesitate to raise your fees, believe me!

The best thing is that, once you're persuaded of the huge value you deliver, your prospective clients will sense that and also connect with you on this new level of confidence you are coming from.

You will state your fees with confidence and never want to charge less for what you do ever again!

How Do You Know You Are Ready to Raise Your Fees?

Many entrepreneurs don't raise their fees, because they are comfortable with what they're earning. But I'd like to caution you: if your business is running well, it's probably not static, but in constant growth. This means it also needs continuing adjustments that have to be made to meet the new challenges that naturally appear with more growth. Otherwise, without realizing it, your growth potential can easily stagnate.

If you have not considered raising your fees, it's preferable to do this sooner than later. Maybe it's time to make an appraisal of what you charge?

Here are three situations that indicate you should raise your fees to boost your income and business growth:

1. **You don't have time to market, because you're too busy working with clients.**
   Marketing is the lifeblood of your business. If you don't have time to advertise yourself because you work too much, then

it's time to up level your clientele. You might lose some clients, but new doors of opportunity leading to better, higher paying clients will open!

2. **People choose you because of your low prices**

   This means your clients know you're a bargain. While haggling over prices may work very well in retail, they are a kiss of death for the small businesswoman. Stop being the cheap option. You don't want to be chosen because you are low-priced, but because your services and results are excellent. Raise your fees and your level and start positioning yourself in the elite category of your market!

3. **You feel in your heart you should give yourself a raise.**

   It is my wish that you get this feeling after reading this chapter. If you recognize you have been charging too little, please don't hesitate to raise your fees! You will not only earn more with the same amount—or even less—of work, you will also step up to a whole new level of confidence and new possibilities for yourself and your business.

Valuable tips to raising your fees:

What I recommend is increasing your rate 20 percent more than what you currently charge.

Make this new offer to your new clients and invite your current customers to jump on the new level of service you offer once the current program they are operating on is finished.

What is Your Time Worth?

Although I don't encourage women who own service-based businesses to charge by the hour, it's important to know if the time you invested in an activity is really worthwhile.

This is easy to calculate:

All you have to do is divide the amount of money you want to pay yourself in one year by the number of hours you want to work. For example:

If you want to pay yourself $5,000 monthly and work 30 hours per week, 50 weeks a year, all you have to do is multiply 5,000 by the number of months (12), and you will obtain your yearly income ($60,000). Then you just have to divide this sum by the number of hours you want to work in a year (30 hours per 50 weeks), which equals 1,500 hours.

$60,000 yearly income divided by 1,500 hours equals $40 per hour.

This way you can use the amount your time is worth to calculate the cost of your time invested in marketing and delivering each offer. This will tremendously help you to become more effective in managing your time, because you'll pinpoint activities that have robbed your time and which you can easily delegate.

Summary Chapter 7: The Confident Queen— How to Own Your Value

- Chronic undercharging is rampant in the female business world, especially among service-based firms, in part because of the discrimination women are still victimized by to a greater or lesser degree. But there are also inner barriers that hold women back from charging more for their services.
- At the core of their being, women are all about helping others. The compassionate and caring female heart will tend to overlook any obstacle that stands between a woman and the possibility to make a difference in another person's life, including her fees.
- You need to create a solid financial structure that allows you not only to stay in business, but to also prosper financially so you will be able to help people as much as you want, without

jeopardizing your future as a successful businesswoman who impacts her community with her talents and expertise.

- Many women compartmentalize their personal finances from all the other areas of their life and are not aware of how money connects to their emotional, mental and physical wellbeing, because they were taught to believe that money and the pursuit of it is a bad thing.

- It is vitally important that the businesswoman understands that pursuing wealth through a business is not only spiritual; it is highly beneficial for the personal development of the woman, which will directly affect her family and her community.

- Women often tend to charge less because they encounter difficulties in choosing their niche market, and because they don't know how to attract new clients or close sales successfully.

- Once you're persuaded of the huge value you deliver, your prospective clients will sense that and also connect with you on this new level of confidence you are coming from.

- Many entrepreneurs are comfortable with what they're earning but they risk stunting the growth potential of their business.

Powerful Action Step:

Step 1: Make a list of at least 30 benefits your clients receive from investing in you, your products and services.

Step 2: Leave that list in a place that is visible for you and read it every day, until you are absolutely convinced of the amazing value you are delivering.

Step 3: Once you are deeply connected to your true worth as a businesswoman, raise your fees by 20%.

—— *Chapter 8* ——

THE AUTHENTIC QUEEN
Goodbye to Miss Perfect

---

ecilia Bravo had to hold back her tears. Here she was—the successful doctor who adamantly defended her patients' rights to solve their health problems with natural remedies and healing—speechless, because her recent patient had expressed her heartfelt gratitude for what she had done for her.

"You saved my life, Doctor Bravo!"

Those words were still ringing in her ears when the patient had finally left her office. Cecilia was puzzled. Why did this client's gratitude trigger these feelings in her?

Cecilia wasn't the crying type of woman. She'd always been resolute and strong, marching ahead as a confident leader, facing the odds that arose when she questioned the status quo in her area of medical expertise.

Yes, she had many conventional adversaries due to her natural approach to medicine, but the great number of successes she had achieved with patients who had not recovered through traditional medicine spoke for itself. What had started as a passion to genuinely help people with what she believed was best for them had turned into a thriving medical practice in the last 10 years.

Yet Cecilia had a hard time acknowledging her achievements. If only she could expand her reach with that website and get more speaking engagements to spread the word about the advantages of natural medicine for diverse ailments. There was still so much that had to get done!

Realizing she had not reached her goals yet, Cecilia sighed. She knew she needed to be more disciplined in order to get the results she wanted and was still light years away from reaching all the lives she desired to impact with her message.

Lives! Her patient had said she had saved her life! Cecilia knew this was not an exaggeration, yet she couldn't acknowledge this achievement. Tears filled her eyes again as she thought about it. How could she ever be good enough?

It was the same question she'd asked herself when she was a little girl. She remembered how she'd often been scolded by both parents, compared to her compliant and cheerful brother Miguel. Her mother, a very quiet and graceful person, had not been able to constrain Cecilia, a curious and strong-willed child who demanded a lot of her attention.

From early on, Cecilia had always pushed the limits, questioning her mother's directions, while Miguel did what he was told and basked in their mama's favor. The result of this was no matter what Cecilia did or did not do in her mother's eyes it was always wrong.

Later, as a teenager, Cecilia sought to gain her parents' recognition by excelling in school. Intelligent, strong and determined she knew she could easily outsmart Miguel. But her parents never seemed to notice that, so very soon she gave up on trying to earn their approval and decided that, one day, she'd become an important person. Then they would finally discover how capable she was!

Then it struck her! Cecilia realized that her patient's words had touched her deeply because they gave voice to the recognition she'd always yearned to hear her parents say.

Yet she still felt that those words did not reflect her true self. She had also made many mistakes in her professional and personal life. In reality, she felt she did not deserve the recognition she received from her patients and some of her colleagues. She was even afraid one day they'd find out she really wasn't the expert she claimed to be.

Never Good Enough

Just like Cecilia, many highly capable and brilliant women feel they are never good enough at what they do, no matter how hard they work or how much they have achieved.

Most of them are not aware of their constant self-doubt, since they have lived with it for most of their lives. But, as a businesswoman, it shows up in a variety of ways:

- Investing more time in a client than planned;
- Allowing too much email access to her personal inbox;
- Giving clients additional benefits they have not paid for;
- Designing customized services and products for each customer;
- Not having clear boundaries with payments from her customers or even providing service to clients who are behind on their payments;
- A lower success rate in her sales conversion;
- Assuming in advance that clients cannot pay and mentally preparing for possible discounts;
- Being quick in letting current clients go;
- Having less confidence in her marketing efforts;

- Shying away from potential clients who question her fees or don't value her products and/or services.

And the list goes on and on.

The truth of the matter is that by not recognizing their achievements, businesswomen turn what could be an enjoyable lifestyle into a busy, self-driven and never-ending quest for perfection in their profession.

Why do women do this to themselves?

If any of the situations I describe above apply to you, you are most likely part of the "Feminine Over-Deliverer Club"—which should not surprise you, since most of us are!

Nevertheless, you won't want to stay that way, because neither your business nor your lifestyle will ever satisfy you as long as you don't learn to restrain from always giving more than intended by empowering your boundaries with the products and services you deliver. The best way to start is by going to the root of the problem.

Why Do You Over-Deliver?

There are many reasons why women are chronic over-deliverers. I'll name some of the causes I've observed in my clients, who tend to stress themselves out for fear of not being good enough.

Please read them carefully to see which one applies to you. It may easily be more than one!

1. Lack of affection:

Many women strive for recognition because they suffered from the lack of love of a primary caregiver, like Cecilia did. Just like in her case, these ladies set very high standards for themselves that are not realistic and make them strive for a level of perfection that often leads them to burn out.

2. Maternal nurturing instincts:

Most women have a natural generosity that includes wanting to protect, nurture and shelter others. Their maternal instincts will lead them to give generously and help others in need, even to the point of sacrificing themselves. Often their feeling of self-worth comes from giving and "being there" for others, at the risk of feeling resentment when their giving is not appreciated.

3. We have a human tendency to mentally disregard ourselves.

It is normal for most human beings, men and women alike, to perceive themselves as "not worthy." The bad consciousness of our "shadow side" makes us believe we're just not as good as others in many areas, including per our professional achievements. A more common term for this feeling of unworthiness is "lack of self-esteem" or "low self-esteem," which is actually the symptom of a deeply rooted perception of our daily failure at being a good person.

Paradoxically, an extreme case of this lack of self-esteem is prevalent in highly successful women: The Impostor Syndrome.

Soon They Will All Know: I'm a Fraud!

Did you know that two out of every five successful people consider themselves to be frauds? And that 70 percent of all people feel like impostors at one time or another?

Even Albert Einstein, the modern day epitome of human intelligence, suffered from feeling like an impostor. A month before his death, he reportedly confided in a friend: "the exaggerated esteem in which my lifework is held makes me very ill at ease. I feel compelled to think of myself as an involuntary swindler."

Strangely enough, this lack of self-recognition is more prevalent among women. Here are some examples of famous women who could easily be categorized as "successful" – but not in their own opinion:

Academy Award-winning actress Meryl Streep: *"You think, 'Why would anyone want to see me again in a movie?' And I don't know how to act anyway, so why am I doing this?"*

Award-winning author Maya Angelou: *"I have written eleven books, but each time I think, 'Uh oh, they're going to find out now. I've run a game on everybody, and they're going to find me out.'"*

Former CEO of Girls, Inc. Joyce Roché: *"Somewhere, deep inside, you don't believe what they say. You think it's a matter of time before you stumble and 'they' discover the truth."*

Famous actress Michelle Pfeifer: *"I still think people will find out that I'm really not very talented. I'm really not very good. It's all been a big sham."*

Oscar-winning actress Kate Winslet: *"Sometimes I wake up in the morning before going off to a shoot, and I think, I can't do this. I'm a fraud."*

Why do successful women doubt their evident level of achievements? It's a strange phenomenon, called the "impostor syndrome."

According to the Caltech Counseling Center, the impostor syndrome is a psychological phenomenon in which people are unable to internalize their accomplishments and are full of chronic self-doubt.

Despite external evidence of their competence, those with this syndrome remain convinced that they are frauds and do not deserve the success they have achieved. Proof of success is dismissed as luck, timing or as a result of deceiving others into thinking they are more intelligent and competent than they believe themselves to really be. It's notable that impostor syndrome is particularly common among high-achieving women.

The Successful Queen Who Never Was

The term "impostor syndrome" first appeared in a 1978 article written by Pauline R. Clance and Suzanne A. Imes observing that many high-achieving women tended to believe they were not intelligent and were over-valued by others.

Imes and Clance found several behaviors of high-achieving women with impostor syndrome. (Clance, Pauline Rose; Imes, Suzanne A., 1978, *The Imposter Phenomenon in High Achieving Women: Dynamics and Therapeutic Intervention,* Psychotherapy: *Theory, Research & Practice* 15 (3): 241–247.)

- **Diligence**: A gifted woman often works hard in order to prevent people from discovering she is an "impostor." This hard work often leads to more praise and success, which perpetuates the "impostor's" feelings and fears of being "found out." The "impostor" woman may feel the need to work two or three times as hard, so overprepare, tinker and obsess over details. This can lead to burn-out and sleep deprivation.

- **Feeling of being phony**: A woman with impostor feelings often attempts to give supervisors and professors the answers that she believes they want, which often leads to an increase in feeling she is **"being a fake."**

- **Use of charm**: Connected to this, gifted women often use their intuitive perceptiveness and charm to gain approval and praise from supervisors and seek out relationships with superiors in order to help her increase her abilities intellectually and creatively. However, when the supervisor gives her praise or recognition, she feels this praise is based on her charm, not on ability.

- **Avoiding display of confidence**: Another way a woman can perpetuate her impostor feelings is to avoid showing any confidence in her abilities. A woman dealing with impostor feelings may believe that if she actually believes in her intelligence and abilities she may be rejected by others. Therefore, she may convince herself she is not intelligent or does not deserve success to avoid rejection.

As you can see, many gifted and talented women feel insecure. You most probably have felt this insecurity when faced with the daily challenges of your life and business.

How Can You Overcome the Impostor Syndrome?

1. Let Go of Perfection

Perfection is the biggest enemy of "good enough." Perfection is insatiable and relentlessly cruel. It dictates unrealistic standards and leads you to imagine that others can meet them, when all along they are just normal people who make all-too-human mistakes, just like you do.

Don't do that to yourself! Go to the root of your drive to feel significant with what you do. In most cases, the root of perfectionism is the need to be loved and accepted.

Well, you are already all of that! You are deeply loved and accepted by God, just as you are, no strings attached.

In a world constantly demanding performance and achievements, it's a concept difficult to understand. Yet it is the essence of God's unconditional love for each and every human being: acceptance and love by grace, not by performance. Given as a gift, even if undeserved, God's love went so far that He made you deserving by making His Son, Jesus Christ, pay for your sins.

Bask in that love, beloved and brilliant businesswoman. In God's eyes you are perfect and loved unconditionally—and that is all that really matters, no matter what anybody else says or thinks about you!

2. Accept That You Play a Vital Role in Your Achievements

Even when you want to explain them away as due to an "unfair" break you had, it was still you who said yes to that opportunity! Give yourself permission to internalize your successes by consciously taking time to celebrate them when you achieve them.

3. Stop Focusing on Yourself

When you put yourself in the center of your world, you become extremely self-conscious and will always fall short and prey to rejection, comparison and insecurity.

You don't have to strive to feel important. You are important. God designed your life with a purpose in mind. He gave you your gifts and talents so you could make a significant contribution to this world and to live handsomely by using them. Don't sabotage your destiny with self-centeredness, because when you do, you rob others of what only you can gift them with.

4. Give Yourself Permission to Fail

Being wrong does not make you a fake. It turns you into a very courageous person who dared to step up and put herself in a position of risk. You're not an impostor for trying something that might not work. You're a heroine!

Charles E. Popplestone wisely said, "Mistakes are the stepping stones to success." This is especially true in the business arena. You can be proud of each one of them, because of everything you learned through them. Being wrong is not failing—it is learning and growing, unless you decide to give up on yourself.

5. Stop playing "Miss Perfect" and Become Vulnerable to Others

By openly admitting your failures and shortcomings you will not be made fun of or be rejected. Vulnerability is a gift to others, since it enables them to connect with you because they identify with your problems and shortcomings. You will not only gain more respect from others, they (and you!) will actually appreciate you more, not less!

At this point you've probably made a conscious decision to cut yourself some slack by internalizing your achievements and are resigned to being perfect. I hope you feel ready to make a powerful step forward, toward a peaceful lifestyle of less stress and more self-appreciation!

However, you may still be asking yourself this nagging question:

If I deliver less, will I earn less?
The answer is no! You can actually earn a lot more by delivering less. By changing your mentality about how you work and implementing business systems that leverage and multiply your time and effort, you can set up a thriving, scalable, 6- or 7-figure business that blesses thousands, with less time and much more fun.

But you will stay stuck in the over-delivery mode if you don't make changes in these three key areas:

Three Steps to Stop Over-delivering:

1. Change Your Mindset: Less is More
The fear of losing clients by reducing the quantity you deliver is a legitimate fear. If you were educated to exchange your hours for dollars, as most of us who come from the traditional school system are, it only sounds logical that you have to give more in order to earn more.

The truth is that there are other amazingly profitable options. The mindset of working more if you want to earn more is just that: a mindset. It is only an idea that has been formed in your head due to the information—or lack of information—you have received until now.

Luckily, mindsets can be changed. All you have to do is educate yourself to think as a businesswoman—instead of as an employee. There are several ways to achieve this:

- Read books written by businesspeople and study how they think and why they do what they do;
- Take courses given by businessmen and -women (caution is advised vis-à-vis academic business schools led by mentors who have never owned a business);
- Have a business mentor who personally guides you to improve your venture;
- Surround yourself with businesspeople. They think differently than people who have jobs working for others. Most of us do not live in close contact with a businessperson, much less a group of them. Try to join a group of businesspeople in your town and meet regularly with them;
- Take imperfect action. Once you have researched and designed a plan, act! I have not seen anything more powerful in terms of educational value for a businessperson than making your own experiences, including your own mistakes. Oh yes, embrace those mistakes! They will be your best teachers!

2. Empower Your Boundaries

One of the most empowering actions you can take is learning the art of setting boundaries.

I learned this the hard way, because I have been a quiet, peaceful person who avoided conflicts, often at any cost. I was brought up in a culture in which it's expected for a woman to be of service to her husband and her family. Combined with low self-esteem and a religious mindset that dutifully embraced a life selflessly lived in the service of others, it was a recipe for disaster in both my personal life and business.

I could not maintain healthy boundaries that defended my own interests. Any time a conflict around borders arose I gave in and let others have their way. This chipped away at my self-esteem, time and finances. Needless to say, it made me feel extremely disempowered. Often I even felt resentment against others, because I was constantly being taken advantage of.

My business made me realize that I was not going to get very far if I did not learn to stand my ground. In this sense, a business can be the most powerful self-development course there is, because you have to learn the art of empowering your boundaries, whether you want to or not. Your numbers will quickly tell you that!

The root of this problem is a lack of self-worth that leads to a bad relationship with money. God showed me through my business that I was being a bad steward of the resources He had put in my hand by not protecting my knowledge, experience, talents, time or money. Wow, when seen from that point of view, what you've been given is sacred!

This astonishing revelation gave me the impulse I needed to stop shortchanging my own worth and to speak from a place of inner confidence, owning my value. It was scary at first, but today I am free from emotional triggers such as guilt, shame or blame when somebody questions my value or asks for more than what was initially programmed. I don't have any more inner conflicts around my boundaries and feel free to take aligned action in every area of my life and business.

Back then I had to learn by trial and error, but you can attack the problem using the powerful action step I'll give you, at the end of this chapter.

3. Delivering in levels

Once you've realized you don't have to work more to earn more and own your worth as a businesswoman who knows how to set and keep healthy boundaries, you are ready to set up your business with a healthy structure that will allow you to deliver amazing value to your clients, earn more money, leverage your time and reach much more people, all at the same time!

The secret of moving from a business that limits its offer to an exclusive group of your clients, to a business that offers diverse products and services that supply the needs of a much broader client base, is delivering in different levels. That way you can multiply your income by transforming one idea into multiple offers.

You basically don't change what you deliver—you only adjust your offer to the current needs and financial commitment levels your clients have.

For example, in a service-based business you can offer a high-level, exclusive service to your elite clients who are willing to fully commit to your high-end programs or services you personally provide to them.

Although this might be the level you are currently working on, you're losing lots of money and robbing many people of your expertise if you don't design additional possibilities for other potential clients, at a lower price point. For example, you design an offer for a group of clients, wherein you might give the same information, but no individual access to you in person.

Another level of delivery could be an online recording of your expertise, method or training with no access to you at all.

Yet another level could be a book or e-book that shares your information.

Each of these echelons is sold at different prices, meeting various clients' needs exactly where they are at the moment.

The magic happens when you integrate these different products and start upselling and down selling from one service to another. Suddenly you will not only earn a given sum per client, but you will see how some clients invest in a variety of your services, multiplying your time, marketing efforts and investments in a huge way!

Once you start delivering in levels, you will smooth out your cash flow while satisfying many more people with your products and services, enabling you to maximize your profit.

Summary Chapter 8: The Authentic Queen— Goodbye to Miss Perfect

- Many highly capable and brilliant women feel they are never good enough at what they do and live in constant self-doubt that jeopardizes the growth of their business.
- The main reasons why women over-deliver are lack of affection, their natural nurturing instincts and our human tendency to mentally disregard ourselves.
- The Impostor Syndrome is a psychological phenomenon in which people are unable to internalize their accomplishments. It is particularly common among high-achieving women.
- The Impostor Syndrome can be overcome by letting go of perfection, accepting your vital role in your achievements, by not focusing on yourself, by giving yourself permission to fail and by becoming vulnerable to others.
- By changing your mentality about how you work and implementing business systems that leverage and multiply your time and effort, you can set up a thriving, scalable, 6- or 7-figure business that blesses thousands, with less time and much more fun.
- To stop over-delivering you have to change your mindset, empower your boundaries and start delivering your expertise at different levels.

Powerful Action Step:

Melt away your tendency to over-deliver with the "Empowering Mindset Breakthrough Handout" from my free workbook: "The

Sleeping Queen's Workbook for Business Women". (You can download it for free at www.TheQueensWorkbook.com)

Chapter 9

THE WISE QUEEN
You Can't Help Everybody

J osefina sighed. It had become so late already! The day had flown by in her busy psychotherapy practice.

Oh well, she said to herself, only one more patient to go and then I'll still have enough time to rush home and tuck Domingo into bed before he falls asleep.

She smiled as she thought of her little boy, while she absentmindedly called in her last patient. Domingo was the apple of her eye. Since the awful divorce from Roberto, it was her son who had kept her from caving in. Every morning Josefina got up to go to work with the sole purpose of providing a better living for both of them.

It had not been easy. Although Josefina did not shy away from work, they were always short of money. It was not that she did not have enough clients. Her practice was growing and she loved to help her patients, but lately she was getting very tired. Somehow more work did not automatically translate into more money, as she expected it should.

Her thoughts drifted back to Domingo. He would probably be eating with his nanny right now. She was already savoring that special moment when she came home and he would run into her arms. Now they were a family of two, but they were a family, alright! If only she could spend more time with him!

"Good evening, doctor!"

Her patient's voice jolted her back to reality. It was Martha, one of her favorite patients, who had sought therapy due to her failing marriage. Josefina was helping her and her husband reignite their marital relationship. The psychotherapist was surprised to see how quickly both of them had recovered their love for each other, after only a few sessions with her.

But this time Martha was not alone—an elderly lady was with her. "My mother," she said. "I'm bringing her with me, because I want her to meet you, so you can help her. She still hasn't recovered from my father's death. I would appreciate it if you recommended what we should do, because her doctor wants her to go to a psychiatrist, but we don't have enough money to pay for that."

The old woman seemed so fragile and her beautiful eyes expressed so much kindness, but also deep sadness. Josefina did not have the heart to tell Martha's mother she had to make a separate appointment to see her.

Martha went into a detailed description of her mother's condition and of how depressed she'd been since her husband passed away. As Josefina listened, deep compassion filled her heart. This poor lady had been through a very difficult time indeed! Josefina immediately started working with Martha's mother. She already knew what to do, since she had successfully helped many of her patients get through the grief and loss of a loved one.

After having a long talk with Martha's mother, Josefina had the impression she was already feeling much better. She remembered them mentioning their financial problems, so she only charged half of her fees. Mother and daughter thanked her profusely for her help and headed towards the door.

What a diverse couple! Josefina realized she had attended to a mourning mother instead of a relationship-troubled daughter. Who will it be tomorrow? In her practice you never knew. Josefina was known among her patients as someone who could adapt quickly to their individual needs and help them in a variety of situations. Many selected her practice because she was empathetic and somehow always managed to fix everybody's problem.

Josefina said a last goodbye to Martha and her mother then glanced at her watch. Oh no! Time had flown by again! She rushed out of her office, hoping she'd still find Domingo awake.

The Hidden Controversy of Serving More People is Better

Since women have a strong sense of solidarity and a deeply supportive nature, they want to help everybody with their expertise. They have a hard time excluding somebody and often negotiate with themselves to include as many people as they can in their niche.

At a first glance, it also makes a lot of sense from the business point of view. If you have a broader market niche, you can help more people and make more money. After all, they reason, if everybody could use your product or services and you limit your market niche, you will get fewer sales.

But is this really so?

Having a bigger market niche may seem to be beneficial for your business, but it really isn't, because you are never seen as an expert and, therefore, never get paid as one.

It's like being a general practitioner who can treat many of his patients' ailments. The GP might be their first choice when they notice the initial symptoms of their sickness, but most will end up seeking out a specialist who has the expertise and reputation for treating their specific malady. The specialist will also be the one who receives the biggest paycheck for the treatment!

Even for a business that is not service-based, it's very important to define your niche, so that you can laser-focus your marketing efforts on that specific segment of your market. No small business marketing budget can survive marketing to a general audience!

That being said, let's define what picking your niche—or "narrowing" it—is really about.

First of all, a niche is more than just picking a segment of people from a certain market so you can start selling them your products and services. A niche has three basic components that will easily distinguish you from anybody else in your market:

1. Your ideal client: somebody who has an urgent need you can supply, is conscious of the need, is willing to solve the problem, values your products and/or services and can pay for them.
2. The problem you solve: your niche has a large variety of problems and needs, but you are the expert who specifically resolves one of them.
3. The method you use to solve the problem: while there may be other experts who offer to solve the same problem for your niche, you have a special way to help them nobody else has.

How Do You Know You Have to Adjust Your Niche?

In my coaching and consulting business I'm always surprised how even very experienced businesswomen who have run their business for many years don't have a definite niche and suffer huge consequences in their business and lives because of it. Josefina, our fictional psychotherapist, is a good example.

You know you need to narrow your niche when:
- You are good at what you do, have a lot of abilities, certificates and experience, yet your clients don't seem to value them;
- You don't get well paid for what you do;
- You are always tired, because you work too hard and too long;
- You are passionate about what you do, but stuck;
- You are confused about your marketing message;
- You have trouble designing your products and services;
- You are marketing yourself, but don't get enough clients.

Although there are plenty of factors that can cause these problems, I've seen with my clients that, more often than not, they have a niche problem when they encounter any of them.

Once they get clear about their niche, they usually gain fresh momentum and start increasing their income.

Here are the advantages of having a specific, well-defined niche in your business:
- It will be much easier for you to position yourself as an expert;
- It will be much easier—and cheaper—to market yourself;
- It will be much easier to design and produce your products and services;
- You will communicate much better with your client, since you'll talk the same language your clients talk;
- You will stand out from your competition;
- You will earn more money.

Common Niching Fears and How to Deal With Them
Normally a combination of the following niching fears will affect the businesswoman:

Fear of having only one niche you will serve for life

I have seen this fear in businesswomen who are in the stage of starting their business. They usually struggle because they have several business ideas and want to implement all of them, under one big umbrella.

That won't work. You cannot help busy mothers educate their children, open a home-based business, organize their time and eat healthy food while cultivating their spiritual life. (Guess how I know? This is the perfect description of my first online business!)

Picking a niche does not mean you'll be stuck with it for life. Of course you can pursue other business ideas as well, but don't do them all at the same time, because you'll spread yourself too thin.

If you have too many business ideas or want to solve too many problems for your client, then you need to do a niche-defining exercise to sort out which one you will start at this phase of your life. (Later in the book I'll explain how to do that.)

Another niching fear is that of over-researching your niche and getting stuck in the infamous analysis-paralysis.

Fear of not defining the niche well enough

In my business I've seen that a niche is not static. As you grow, your business grows and your niche is refined in the process. So don't worry if you are starting out and don't have your niche 100 percent figured out yet. It will get clearer as your business grows.

I always tell my new clients who are still insecure about their niche even after going through the necessary research and exercises to define it: "don't worry, start working and your niche will find you!"

The truth is, your clients will help you narrow your niche. You will notice what exact profile of a person has the best results with you, what problem you're best at solving, whom you're more passionate about helping and serving and who most values your services and products and is really willing to pay for what you do.

Fear of losing money and clients

This fear is obvious. I have seen that most women start to negotiate within themselves when they want to narrow—or completely change—their niche: They don't want to leave their former clients out!

The first thing they have to realize is this fear comes from their past business experiences that only got them this far. For these businesswomen it's as if they're denying services to somebody asking for help that they can provide. In reality, you are allowing the people you can help best to access solutions to the problems you are brilliant at solving.

Your former clients either did:

- Not have that need;
- Or they did have the need, but were not conscious of it;
- Or they were conscious of it, but were not willing to change the situation;
- Or they were willing to change the situation, but did not value your services;
- Or they valued your services, but did not have the money to pay you.

Believe me, you don't want to work with a client who meets any of those conditions, even if you have gotten used to them over the past years!

Your fear of losing customers stems from a deeper fear: not trusting that there really is something better for you.

Of course there is! God would not have given your gifts and talents so that you have to work yourself to death without ever having great results!

There are enough money and clients out there for you! Just trust God and dare to go and look for them! Start believing in God's best for you and your business and prepare the ground, so your future ideal client will recognize you once you market yourself to him or her!

Fear of leaving your comfort zone

When I work with clients to help define their niche, I inspire them to look beyond what they're used to. I do that because frequently I see them trapped in a niche that is comfortable and familiar to them, but not profitable enough to guarantee a thriving income for them. I challenge them to contemplate different markets they've never considered, who will gladly invest in my client's expertise once she dares to make an offer to them.

For example, a life coach can help immigrants adjust to their new surroundings because she herself is an immigrant and feels deeply connected to that niche, due to her own experiences.

But she could make much more money if she switches to a more lucrative client. (Hello! Immigrants often have to start from scratch and don't have the money to pay a coach.) For example: executives who have been transferred from another country and face the challenges of holding corporate leadership positions as foreigners. She could even offer her services to international companies who often deal with the problems of having multi-cultural staffs.

Can you see how a change of niche can skyrocket your business? This coach might be intimidated by the high position of her new client and even feel inadequate, because she does not have a corporate background, but, the truth is, she doesn't have to! All she needs to be is a brilliant coach who helps them navigate their own world of daily new challenges successfully, by adapting the same methods she used with her former clients, the immigrants.

The big difference for the coach will be in her bank account, that's for sure!

Fear of making a definite decision

The key word is "definite." It means you will choose from several GOOD options that will most probably affect your future and that of your company for an extended period of time. Scary, I know! That's why some businesswomen are very anxious about making decisions, especially when they're just starting out.

Decision-making is a very important skill for a businessperson and leader. It's not easy, but who said it would be? It's the reason why many people don't strive to become leaders: because they don't want to assume the huge responsibility of making decisions.

So, how do you make good, quick and definite decisions?

First you have to get clear about your options and your priorities. Often businesswomen cannot make decisions, because they simply don't have enough information to make informed choices. Or they might have the information, but are not 100 percent clear about their priorities.

Once you've gathered the necessary information and established priorities, you will be clear about your options and it will be much easier to decide which way to go.

It is no different for niching. Do the homework and research your potential markets. Get a good mentor to help you determine your niche. Do what it takes to define your niche as precisely as you can.

Then, when you are ready to decide... decide!

Once You've Decided, How Do You Change Your Niche?

Many clients whom I helped to define a new niche—or narrow their existing niche—didn't know how to go about transitioning over to a new niche after working with a certain segment of the market that was not ideal for them.

My suggestion is to make it short and sweet. Don't undergo an agonizingly long transition that will only confuse you and your clients, old and new. Tell everybody about it through your habitual messaging channels and then just switchover and start targeting your new client with laser-focused marketing, as fast as you can.

How to Find a Highly Profitable Niche

I've witnessed how powerful it is for many of my clients to attain clarity about the exact niche that is being served. Once you know exactly who your ideal client is, what particular problems you solve and how you can uniquely meet their needs, you'll become unstoppable!

That is why niche-determining is one of my favorite exercises I do with clients, because it brings them into motion very quickly. I call it my "3D Niche Defining Exercise."

The 3D Niche Defining Exercise:

Discover Your Brilliance, Define Your Potential and Distinguish Your Options

What I most love about this exercise is that it teaches you to approach your market from a very different angle than most people do. From my own experience, I see that most people first look at what they have to offer and then they go out into the market to see whom they can sell it to. Although it sounds reasonable, it is not the best approach, because you will very often find that you and your market don't speak the same language at all.

What you see as a need is not necessarily seen as a necessity by them. Or they may express it differently. Potential clients might not recognize that your proposal is the solution to their problem (even if it is!), because you see it from a different standpoint than they do. Keep in mind that you already know what the solution is, while in their head, they're still struggling with the problem and may think that the solution looks quite different. Even if they're wrong, they will not buy from you as long as they're looking for other ways to solve their problem.

I know it sounds very confusing and that's why this exercise beautifully simplifies the process of determining how to communicate what to sell and whom to sell it to.

Basically, what you have to do is to go out into the market, pick a category of people who have a high potential of becoming good clients, study them and then look at what you have in your hand to adjust to their specific situation and requirements.

When you pick categories, don't just stay in the one you are most comfortable with. Dare to contemplate new genres you've never worked with. You'll be surprised to see what you find!

Once you've chosen a few categories, define several potential ideal clients in that sphere. For example, if you choose the fast growing category of small businesses/entrepreneurs, you can sub-divide it into several profiles of ideal clients:

- A mother who wants to build a business from home;
- A local business owner who wants to expand his/her reach online;
- A consultant who wants to leave his/her job and become independent.

As you can see, each one of these represent a potential niche you will want to research separately.

For each one of them you can ask yourself:

- What are the problems they experience daily?
- What emotions do they feel daily?
- What solutions are they looking for?
- What do they need to do, learn or know?
- Why do they desire to change?
- What is the outcome they're looking for?

Once you've deliberated and answered all of these questions for each niche you have picked, then you still must consider the number of people in each niche, their culture, their tendency to solve the problem, their willingness to invest in solving similar problems and the appreciation you have for that client.

When you've gone through all these "filters," you will be much clearer on the options you have and will be ready to choose your ideal client and problems you'll solve.

All you have to do now is decide which one to pick and you're done!

Summary Chapter 9: The Wise Queen— You Can't Help Everybody

- Having a bigger market niche may seem to be beneficial for your business, but it really isn't, because you are never seen as an expert and, therefore, never get paid as one.

- A niche has three basic components that will easily distinguish you from anybody else in your market: your ideal client, the problem you solve, and the method you use to solve the problem.

- Once you know exactly who your ideal client is, what particular problems you solve and how you can uniquely meet their needs, you'll become unstoppable!

- Picking a niche does not mean you'll be stuck with it for life. Of course you can pursue other business ideas as well, but don't do them all at the same time, because you'll spread yourself too thin.

- A niche is not static. As you grow, your business grows and your niche is refined in the process.

- Many women fear losing money and clients when they narrow their niche, because they think they're denying services to somebody asking for help that they can provide. In reality, they are allowing the people they can help best to access solutions to the problems they are brilliant at solving.

• Decision-making is a very important skill for a businessperson and leader. Often businesswomen cannot make decisions, because they simply don't have enough information to make informed choices. Or they might have the information, but are not 100 percent clear about their priorities.

Powerful Action Step:

Complete The 3D Niche Defining Exercise: "Discover Your Brilliance, Define Your Potential and Distinguish Your Options" in my complimentary workbook. (Download my free workbook: "The Sleeping Queen's Workbook for Business Women" at www. TheQueensWorkbook.com)

---- *Chapter 10* ----

THE COMPASSIONATE QUEEN
How to Reach Those You Were Called to Help

C hristina sensed a shiver go down her spine. There it was again, the same feeling she had every time she lifted up the phone to ask for an interview at the radio station. She did not have to deliberate long about where this feeling came from. It was sheer terror to her! Having to talk to somebody who clearly did not know who she was, to convince him or her to do an interview she herself was not convinced should be done, was clearly the worst aspect of her business.

She loved coaching, was passionate about helping clients and great at delivering value to them. Christina could spend hours designing her coaching programs and writing articles for career women about how to live a stress-free life while still excelling at their job.

But she hated the marketing piece of her business. She always seemed to run up against a wall when she tried to connect with a possible speaking opportunity or even a joint venture partnership with fellow coaches.

All she ever heard was either a straight "No, not interested" or "Please call us in the future." When she wrote emails it was even worse, because she received no answer at all, just silence, which forced her to reconnect with that person, with that gnawing feeling in her gut that he or she was not interested.

Christina could not help feeling rejected and undervalued when she marketed herself. It was painful to experience how irrelevant the topic she was so passionate about seemed to be to everybody except her.

Yet she knew she had to do it! If she did not work on her visibility, it would be impossible for her business to grow. She also did some social media and even hired somebody to do paid publicity, budget permitting, but she knew it was not enough.

If she could only get an interview on a renowned radio channel or a well-positioned joint venture with a co-partner who could introduce her to his or her world, then she would quickly be able to position herself in front of a lot of people!

But how could she feel more confident when trying to persuade them? Christina wondered if she would ever be able to do that. Right now she could not even look at the phone without feeling anxious about being rejected once again.

How does everybody else do this? She remembered a video in which a marketing expert said how enjoyable marketing was to him. Really? Christina could not remotely imagine how such an ordeal could ever be fun for anybody.

Then she remembered her monthly income goal. If she did not get more clients now, she would barely make it through the month!

She took a deep breath and reached for the phone. In front of her was the script she had written down, word for word, what she would say. This time she ignored the ominous feeling that came over her every time she picked up the phone and dialed the number.

Women and Marketing

Based on my years of helping women entrepreneurs excel at their business I can see most have very similar reactions to Christina when it comes to making the necessary connections for gaining a higher profile.

Most women shy away from seeking out opportunities to position themselves as celebrities. They usually require lots of coaching and reaffirmation before they face a prospective client or possible joint venture partner. I have even heard from women who are already well-positioned who hate marketing.

Why?

Although there's no evidence of gender bias in the marketing arena, I do believe women can encounter greater difficulties than men do when they try to increase their market positioning.

One of the reasons is that, in many cultures, success comes at a greater price for a woman than for a man. Since the business realm has been historically dominated by men, very often women tend to be categorized as "masculine" when they gain success in business.

This causes some women to be less aggressive when it comes to marketing themselves. Unconsciously, they are afraid of betraying their feminine values.

Other than that, there are two basic fears that keep men and women alike from becoming good at gaining visibility and marketing themselves:

- The fear of speaking in public;
- The fear of rejection.

Both fears are reported to be the greatest fears a person can ever experience, even above the fear of dying. No wonder so many women struggle with their marketing!

How Do You Deal With Marketing Fears?

I think one of the most important things is to learn not to take a "no" as a personal rejection. Don't blame yourself when you get a no. Most often it is more of a "not now" or "not this." For example, if you're inquiring about doing an interview and don't get a yes, ask if they would be interested in the future or what they would really like to feature in their program.

Contemplate your "no's" as part of the process. It would be unrealistic to get 10 yeses out of ten applications interview requests, right? From this point of view, getting a "no" is just part of the marketing process. As you do this over and over again, try to define your success ratio, for example, one "yes" out of every 10 calls—then expect to get those nine "no's".

After receiving a "no," keep the conversation going. Follow up after a few months and check to see if they are interested. Perseverance is crucial. I experienced that with a TV station I wanted to be on. The first time I called, I got a "maybe, sometime…" which, in the Hispanic culture, is a polite way of saying no. But I kept calling until they eventually told me they would get in touch with me if an opportunity arose. Again, they never did.

After a few months passed I called them again. I found out the former person in charge had left, which was why they had not called me back. Soon after that we made an appointment and I finally landed in front of their cameras! If I'd assumed they'd never put me on the air and had not called back, I would have lost that opportunity!

Another important strategy for increasing one's profile is to have a marketing routine. I market 30 minutes every day in a very organized fashion. I research possible connections and record everything I do on an Excel sheet. That way I can quickly review whom I last connected with, when and what their last response was. I have all their contact information there, so I can easily follow up. This way you just keep on planting seeds, every day a little bit here and a little bit there. Eventually those seeds start bearing fruit!

Another tip is to constantly put yourself out there in a less aggressive manner. Don't just market yourself directly. Position yourself by delivering great content through your website, social media and/ or newsletter. That way you'll practice being visible in a powerful way, which is also much more comfortable for you than grabbing the phone to connect directly with one person. You'll be sharing your expertise with the general public or a target market from behind your computer or mobile phone.

Rejection can quickly lead to isolation. Be aware that you're not the only one struggling with marketing. Every businessperson has to overcome rejection one time or another. That's why it's crucial for you to keep in touch with fellow businesswomen who are going through and struggling with the same issues you are.

Celebrate yourself! Every yes you get is a trophy to treasure. Keep it in front of your eyes in a visible way, as a hallmark of your success in gaining visibility, so that you never forget you CAN do this!

What has most helped me to persevere in my marketing efforts is that my business is really not about me.

It's Not About You, It's About Them

My business has never been just a means for making money. I don't think it is for anybody in the market. I believe entrepreneurs are called to the marketplace with a passion that is God-given, so they can make significant contributions to their community with their talents and gifts.

You might never have thought of your business in this way, but you probably felt a deep passion when you started out. Of course, you wanted it to financially thrive, otherwise it would not be a business, but you also were pursuing deeper values, like freedom, prosperity, a lifestyle and personal satisfaction.

Those desires come directly from God. He deeply loves you and desires you to be prosperous, free and fulfilled, more than even you do for yourself!

But once you are prosperous and free, you'll desire to share whatever you achieve with others. You will recognize that money and freedom in and by themselves won't fulfill you.

That's why famous millionaires end up becoming philanthropists, making important contributions to their community. The reason why is very simple: we're created in God's image and are, essentially givers, like He is.

This essence of human nature is the divine in us. Many times it is smothered by a scarcity mentality which comes from our surroundings, culture, media and education, but deep down inside, we know that doing without is not God's plan for us and that we are called to be blessed and to be a blessing to others. This deeply ingrained desire to give our lives a purpose by being a blessing to others flourishes in many ways.

One of them is through business. Without even considering the romantic view of making a difference in other people's lives, a business is morally one of the best things you can do! Businesses keep the world's economies running, provide job opportunities for others and are the prime movers for human creativity and innovation.

I hope you have become aware of the importance of your business, which reaches far beyond your own little domain. Once you grasp this fact, becoming visible should not be an issue anymore, because it is not about you anymore. It is about the people you can reach with your message, the difference you can make with your product, the jobs you can give, the lives that will change, etc.

From this point of view, it is almost a responsibility to get your marketing message out there. Can you see this? Every time you have to pick up that phone to make a marketing connection, think of those people you were called upon to influence with your business. I can assure you those calls will never be the same again to you!

How to Quickly Position Yourself as an Expert in Your Market

As you can imagine, this topic goes beyond the scope of this book—it's so broad several volumes could be written about it! So, what I'll do is share a thing or two about the visibility-mindset and what has best worked for me.

Visibility, as everything else in your life, starts inside of you. Once you are clear about what visibility is for you in the deepest core of your being, it will only manifest naturally for you on the outside.

If you don't do the "inside job" first, you will try to have results by forcing them to happen outwardly, like Josefina, our fictional coach who was cold-calling for an interview. She was trying to do what she thought was right, but everything inside of her cringed at picking up that phone.

Whenever you encounter this controversy as a businesswoman (which you most certainly will!), listen to your body, feelings and intuition! They are trying to tell you something. If you take the time to process your challenges from the inside out, you will be amazed at the clarity you will get about how to handle your business. What can seem to be an insurmountable task can become something you almost do naturally when you align your spirit, identity and beliefs before taking action.

Your Spirit and Your Visibility

As I explained above, my "Big Why" is what has helped me more than anything to overcome shyness and fear of rejection and to get out there to be seen. Throughout all the years as a businesswoman, my "Big Why" is what has kept me going.

It has taken my eyes off myself and focused on the lives I can impact with what the Lord has put in my heart to do. This may be scary sometimes, because God is a big thinker, and the vision He puts in our hearts can be overwhelming, yes, even impossible.

But, at the same time, it's a relief, because right from the get-go you can give up at trying to achieve it by yourself. Instead of carrying that burden and goal around with you and getting overwhelmed by the sheer thought of it, you can choose to rest in God's grace and let Him do the job.

Does that mean you don't work on your project? By no means! Of course you will do what it takes, but without worry and stress, trusting in God's divine provision for everything you need to accomplish.

That includes your efforts to become visible. Believe me, it is much easier to pick up that phone when you know God's favor is on your life and that He Himself is backing you up and opening doors no man can close!

This is a verse He gave me the day He announced my calling to the business world to me:

"I know your works. See, I have set before you an open door, and no one can shut it; for you have a little strength, have kept My word, and have not denied My name."

– *Revelation* 3:8

Take a moment to write down what your "Big Why" is. Ask yourself:

- WHY am I doing what I'm doing?
- Why is this important to me?

Write down whatever comes to your mind. Don't worry if it does not come out in the right words. Just brainstorm whatever comes to you. Then you can still polish it up as God gives you new revelations about His purpose for your life.

If you've never asked yourself a similar question, don't panic if nothing significant comes up! It's not like God would give everybody a perfect plan for their lives and missed out on you! Take your time and meditate on this. Ask God for revelation. He will tell you, in your heart!

Once you have your "Big Why", you will understand why becoming visible is so important to achieve that goal!

Your Identity and Your Visibility

Once you are clear about your "Big Why" for your business, you can move to the next level of your innermost being: your identity.

Who are you thinking of yourself as?

Go back to your "Big Why" and imagine you are already living it.

Who are you in your "Big Why"?

Whatever comes up at this level might seem way too impossible for you right now, but you better get used to it, because that is how God sees you: victorious, accomplished and successful!

Your Beliefs and Your Visibility

To attain the new identity that walks in your "Big Why", what would you have to believe to make this possible?

What are your beliefs right now? Are they in conflict with what you want to achieve for your life?

What if these conflicting beliefs were no longer important to you?

Write down your "Big Why," your identity and your beliefs and read them out to yourself every day. Start internalizing them as your truth about yourself. Adopt this as your default mindset about yourself. Don't allow your thoughts to drift back to your former way of seeing yourself.

Now you can make your decisions from who you are going to be then, not who you are right now. You can allow yourself to think big.

You can make a plan of the outcomes you want to achieve for your business and the actions you need to take to get you there.

Now you are ready to get visible!

Five Ways to Quickly Position Yourself as an Expert in Your Market
Although it's true that some people seem to be born with the charisma and natural leadership skills that are necessary to stand out from the crowd, I can assure you that lasting visibility for a business has little to do with that.

Being an introvert myself, I used to struggle with the thought of being more "out there." In my eyes I was just not "that type of person." Of course, that was before I knew this was more of a mindset than a genetic issue. Now, as I look back, I realize that visibility is just another aspect of your business you can very naturally integrate into everything you are already doing.

For example, at first I was not very keen on standing in the limelight, but I was consistent, I loved my message and was passionate about what I was doing. This sensibility suffused everything I did, starting with my newsletters, articles, messages and some occasional interviews. Over time I noticed that I actually was standing out from the crowd, even above people who were much "noisier" about themselves, because I was always there. That gave me huge credibility, something I still enjoy to this day. Many of my clients come to me because they trust me, because of my consistency. As Woody Allen said: "90 percent of life is showing up."

Was it the right way to get visible? Definitely not! Passion is wonderful, but in your business you have to couple it with effective planning and strategy in order to advance it. I would have positioned myself much quicker had I coupled this one aspect of visibility with the other four I will show you below. But it does get the point across that for a businesswoman an effective public presence is intimately linked to her credibility and one doesn't work without the other.

So don't plan on becoming a shooting star; rather, plan to do your business with integrity, passion and love. And then get the habit of talking about it whenever and wherever you can!

That way being visible is really easy, because it's not just a necessary compartment of your business, but a natural part of everything else you do.

What Does This Look Like in Your Day-To-Day Business Life?
Here are five areas you are probably already working on that you can easily exploit far more to gain credibility and visibility for your business.

1. Share Your Growth Openly
You have read this book because you are passionate about your business. You like looking to the future and aiming at that vision God has put in your heart and you are willing to stretch, grow and face the challenges that come your way to make it happen.

Please be aware that this attitude places you in the ranks of only 3 percent of the world's population! 97 percent of people would like to change their situation, but are not necessarily willing to do it or they don't dare to.

My point is that just being a feminine entrepreneur already positions you as a leader in your field. Now go out there and share your growth process and leadership with others! Tell them about the courses you're taking, other businesspeople you network with and who your mentor is.

Talk about how you are always on the go and what you are planning in order to further your business even more. I promise, that will catch people's attention!

You can also mention the people in your circle who are already growing with you. Talk about your clients, share what you are teaching them, highlight their results and celebrate their growth too.

2. Do Your Best

I know I don't have to tell you that. To me businesswomen are the most admirable and brilliant people when it comes to commitment and delivering quality.

But are you talking about it, getting the word out?

Not talking about it is not modesty! Remember your "Big Why"? How will the people who need to hear your message or buy your products ever believe in what you do if you yourself cannot openly acknowledge it?

Don't just set high standards for yourself, talk publicly about the high value you deliver. Give current and potential clients the expectation of having a high quality experience every time they contact you. Don't be afraid of taking personal pride in what you do. That way you powerfully own your worth and other people will pick up on that!

Another way of doing this is by giving useful tips when talking about what you do, at meetings, teleseminars, interviews, networking and the like. Grab the microphone whenever you can and ask awesome questions, so everybody can acknowledge you're an expert who clearly knows what she's doing. Don't forget to introduce yourself:

"My name is _____, from www._____.com, author of the book _____. My question is:…"

Be generous with your knowledge whenever you have the opportunity to give handouts. Include "done-for-you" material, checklists, templates, step-by-step formulas, fill-in-the- blank exercises, etc. This will become part of your branding and whenever your name comes up people will see you as the entrepreneur who "goes the extra mile" to deliver great value.

Take advantage of the media. Be willing to get interviewed and quoted in magazines. You can submit your articles to publications in your field and contact journalists who might be interested in what you do. Keep in touch with them if they don't cover you right away and be ready when they do. Show that you are available at a moment's notice by having a press kit available to anybody who is from the media and shows interest in what you do.

Win an award. That may be something you have never thought of, because you might believe it is totally beyond your grasp. That is what happened to me until one of my dear mentors told me that one reason why I don't win awards is because I never apply. So I started applying for several awards. Initially, I didn't receive any, but I was persistent. Long story short: it worked! I won an Apex Award for Publication Excellence in the Electronic Media - Education & Training category in 2015! It felt really rewarding and special, plus it greatly enhanced my credibility in my field of expertise and in general.

How do you apply for awards? At *www.Google.com* search for awards in your fields, for instance "business awards." Get into the habit of applying regularly. Don't get dissuaded if you don't win at first. If there is an award you'd really like to win, try to contact the entity offering the award and ask specifically what their judges most value and are looking for in a winner. Then go and get yourself an award!

3. Display Your Results

As you progress provide constant proof that you are not only on the ball, but also have amazing results! Talk about your clients regularly. You can share pictures showing you working with them or of special "Aha" moments that led to special breakthroughs for those who retain your services. Social media offers excellent platforms for this.

Make sure to ask every client for a testimonial. You can make this easier for them by preparing a special readymade template, so all clients really just have to do is fill in the blanks when they provide their testimonial.

This can be personalized: often I myself write a testimonial based on comments a satisfied customer has made to me verbally or via email.

Then I send this endorsement based on their statements back to them asking for permission to publish it. When I work personally with clients I also ask for video-testimonials.

You can also share the results of your business: how long you have been operating; awards your venture has received; number of articles that have been published; newsletters sent to subscribers; clients worked with; conferences given; testimonials; etc.

Don't assume people know your numbers or how long your business has been in existence. Mention it as often as you can!

4. Embrace Your Leadership Role Fully

People have a very basic desire to belong. They yearn to be part of something bigger than their own individual selves. You can create that for them! You can generate a world that likeminded people feel safe to be a part of. This is what leaders do. You are an agent of change. You have already stepped out of the crowd to make a difference. To bring a different option to the table: your option!

Don't ever disconnect from that greatness God has put inside you. I cannot overemphasize this, because you will often receive messages intended to tear you down and discourage you, such as "flaming" by Internet trolls who usually hide behind their online anonymity. You're likely to receive challenges in your business that may make you feel insignificant and unqualified! Expect lots of demeaning messages from your environment.

I will talk more about that later, but for now be aware that you will have to fight to keep yourself 100 percent conscious of the huge difference you have been divinely called upon to make. God summoned you to be a businesswoman because He believes in you and that you are able to do it.

You might not always feel you measure up to that, but that is a good thing, because it makes you dependent on God and on His grace to get the job done. God may not always call the qualified, but He always qualifies those He calls!

Knowing this frees you to truly dream big, envisioning something much bigger than your separate self. You can choose to trust that God's supernatural power is going to get the job done. That's what faith is all about!

Part of fully stepping into your leadership role as a businesswoman is using the words that describe your world as something that is exclusive and different. Describe whatever you do with words like: rare, VIP, elite, exclusive, trendsetting, etc.

Elicit action from others intended to make them become part of your world. Show them that being part of what you do cannot be taken for granted. Share your numbers. Announce how many people took action, signing up for your courses and events. Share how taking action changed your business. If something is sold-out, let the world know!

Share how other people reach out to you and how you connect to them. Mention how somebody who is important in your field addressed you, or said something important that impacted you.

5. Be Your Own Cheerleader

After having described the previous four ways to gain visibility with the goal of getting you into the habit of magnifying, communicating and sharing what you are already doing, I will invite you to take one more step: allow yourself to become a star!

Allow that celebrity part of you to come alive, even if you are a bashful, low profile person. Again, don't just think of yourself, but of all the people you can reach by gaining more exposure and God's plan for you!

Look and dress well. When you go to events, get photographed with the event leader. Most of them will gladly have a picture taken with you. Always have a cell phone handy to snap a selfie with noteworthy people you want to be associated with. Follow up with them later by sending them the picture and thanking them for the event. Offer them a testimonial, they'll be thrilled.

Write your own book and self-publish it. Seek out the best endorsements you can possibly get. Be polite and respectful, but persistent, when asking for endorsements.

One Last Word About Your Environment

Being visible takes a lot of courage. That's why your environment is so crucial in supporting you and your business. It will be much more difficult for you to project yourself as a successful businesswoman if you come from a place of chaos in your team, schedule or physical environment.

You don't have to have everything together, but by all means, take a closer look at your surroundings and ask yourself how you can improve it to feel supported by it?

What I have seen very often is that businesswomen are in a state of perpetual personal growth, which can be challenging for the people around them. When you get excited about your business' next step it's highly likely that most people around you won't have a clue what's happening in your life and will therefore not be supportive, unless you take the time to explain it to them. You have to understand that, as far as they're concerned, you are still where you used to be. Very often stagnant, complacent people don't realize you have changed, because they're still stuck in the same rut or routine. Some will resist your change—even feel threatened by it, often reacting like total buzzkills.

I have seen that, in these situations, many times all you have to do is ask for more help and support. At other times the decision is more difficult, since it requires your letting go of someone or something that is holding you back.

Take the time to genuinely ask yourself: as a highly successful businesswoman who is an expert in her field, what do I need to ask for? What do I need to let go of?

Be vigilant and maintain surveillance over your own little world and protect it. Ideally it should be your haven, a place where you get edified, not depleted of your energy.

Summary Chapter 10: The Compassionate Queen— How to Reach Those You Were Called to Help

- The fear of speaking in public and the fear of rejection keep men and women alike from becoming good at gaining visibility and marketing themselves.
- Don't take a "no" personally. Most often it is more of a "not now" or "not this."
- A business is morally one of the best things you can do! Businesses keep the world's economies running, provide job opportunities for others and are the prime movers for human creativity and innovation.
- Becoming visible is not about you. It is about the people you can reach with your message, the difference you can make with your product, the jobs you can give, the lives that will change, etc.
- Visibility, as everything else in your life, starts inside of you. Once you are clear about what visibility is for you in the deepest core of your being, it will only manifest naturally for you on the outside.
- Being visible takes a lot of courage. That's why your environment is so crucial in supporting you and your business. It will be much more difficult for you to project yourself as a successful businesswoman if you come from a place of chaos in your team, schedule or physical environment.

Powerful Action Step:

What can seem to be an insurmountable task can become something you almost do naturally when you align your spirit, identity and beliefs before taking action.

Take a moment to write down your "Big Why", your identity and your beliefs by answering the powerful coaching questions for this chapter in my free workbook: "The Sleeping Queen's Workbook for Business Women" (You can download it for free at www.TheQueensWorkbook.com)

Chapter 11

THE WEALTHY QUEEN

The Businesswoman and Her Money

The sound of the dripping water was driving Miriam mad. As much as she enjoyed living in the old log cabin, she was getting tired of the leaking roof. Every time it rained she found a new hole that had to get fixed. She sighed. They would have to wait till summer to get that done... if they had the money!

She stared out of the window while vigorously kneading the bread on her kitchen table. Right now, all she could see was the rain pouring steadily on the green grass outside. Their chickens were perched on the branches of an old tree, patiently waiting for the rain to pass and their playful puppy, Samuel, was barking at the ducks again, who were oblivious of the pouring rain around them as they waddled into the small homemade pond they had made with the children. Everything was grey and wet, yet wonderfully alive, at the same time!

Miriam forgot about the leak in the roof as her thoughts drifted back to the day they had bought this old house. After their daughter Sandra's

152

last asthma attack, both Miguel and she finally made the decision to leave the big city behind to seek a quieter life in the countryside.

They'd grown tired of the incessant busyness of their crazy life in corporate America and resolved to homeschool their three children and raise them in healthier, more natural surroundings. "Back to a simpler life" was their mantra. They were going to leave materialism behind to pursue a life grounded on what really mattered: God, marriage and family.

When they were offered this old log cabin it was like a dream come true for them. It had a beautiful setting, surrounded by a dense forest with a view on a pristine lake, the majestic mountains reflected in its peaceful waters. A perfect place to raise children and connect with nature again!

Miguel very soon found a job only ten minutes away at the Lakeside Hotel and Miriam was busy providing several area spas with delectable gluten-free products from her bakery. They were not earning nearly what they had earned in the city, but it seemed worthwhile. Besides, money was not important. She had already experienced the price they had to pay for a more affluent lifestyle and she no longer desired to return to the rat race.

The honking Mercedes Benz brought her back to reality.

"Oh, so she did come!" Miriam thought, cleaning her hands from the sticky bread dough.

It was her neighbor, Giovanna, owner of the Italian Restaurant, who wanted to learn how to bake gluten-free pizza. Miriam could not help but smile as she watched Giovanna bustle out of her luxurious car and struggle to open her umbrella as she quickly strutted across the muddy yard in her high heels. What a sight! She definitely looked out of place in their old farmyard.

Although they were so different, Miriam deeply admired her neighbors. Giovanna and her husband were a buoyant couple, descendants of Italian immigrants, who had built a chain of Italian restaurants in their lake area, literally from nothing.

As she stepped into their home, Giovanna displayed her usual confidence by throwing off her coat and affectionately hugging Miriam, while incessantly talking and explaining her delay. Today, as always, she looked stunning, as if she had stepped straight out of a Hollywood movie. Giovanna's voice was full of excitement. She had just purchased a new piece of land for another restaurant and one of her sons was going to run it!

Miriam wondered how everything Giovanna touched seemed to turn to gold. She attracted money like a magnet. What really intrigued her was how happy Giovanna always seemed to be. Did she ever get stressed out by her busy lifestyle?

Her question was immediately answered as Giovanna spurted out how they were going to Italy next week to celebrate their wedding anniversary. The next 30 minutes flew by as Giovanna shared the exciting details of their trip while Miriam barely managed to explain how to prepare and bake her recipe for gluten-free pizza.

Before she knew it, Giovanna was already fumbling into her raincoat again. She profusely thanked Miriam for the recipe, dropped a generous amount of dollars into her hand, floated out of the room—and Miriam's existence.

As Giovanna's Mercedes hummed off in the distance, Miriam suddenly felt nostalgic. As she looked around their log cabin she could still smell Giovanna's expensive perfume in the air. Wow, Italy! She tried to picture herself travelling to Europe. How wonderful would that be?

But her imaginary trip quickly evaporated as the dripping sound of the roof leak brought her back to reality again. Right now, Italy was out of the question for them. They were lucky if they could fix that roof this summer! Miriam rolled up her sleeves and started kneading her bread again.

Money Affects Everything

Money is a fascinating subject. After trying to ignore it for almost all my life, I finally started to confront myself and my beliefs around money when I discovered how much they affected my life, business and clients. Duh! I know, it might sound obvious, but you would be surprised if you knew how many women entrepreneurs don't know how to properly relate to money!

Back then I decided to dive deep into this contentious topic that I had tried to avoid for much too long. I knew that if I could heal my own relationship with money, I could also help others to accomplish this.

It took me a year to get certified in two life-changing coaching methods that have forever transformed the way I relate to money and literally revolutionized my coaching practice: "The Sacred Money Archetypes" and the "Money Breakthrough Method" devised by Kendall Summerhawk.

It never ceases to amaze me how much money affects our lives and how little we, as women, are actually aware of it. Most women have a bad relationship with money, because they were taught to believe that money and the pursuit of it is a bad thing.

The result is that they cultivate a bad relationship with money, because they choose to deny the importance that money has in their lives. They compartmentalize their personal finances, separating this from all other areas of life.

Women are not aware of how money connects to their emotional, mental and physical stress level, which not only directly affects her family's wellbeing but even causes the vast majority of marriage problems and divorces.

We love to say that money is not important, but the truth is, it touches every single area of our life! And because it is intimately connected to every aspect of our lives, money should be given the place of importance and respect it deserves to have.

Believe me, if you try to deny its significance, it will demand that you pay attention to it—whether you like it or not! Money needs to be taken good care of in our lives, given its proper due and put in its rightful place in everything we do.

Once you start taking steps in that direction, you will also start noticing changes in your money story!

If you are a woman entrepreneur and you are having conflicts around money, it's highly probable you have reached a certain income level you cannot surpass. Without realizing it you may even be psychologically imposing your own internalized "glass ceiling" upon yourself.

That is exactly what happened to me when I started out with my online business in 2007. I began to share my message with a lot of passion, but did not pay attention to what I was or was not earning. I was totally disconnected from my own numbers!

As you can imagine, the result was that my business did not prosper at all. I made a certain amount of money, but never met my financial goals. I very soon realized that if I didn't master this area of my business, I was not going to get very far!

My Money Story: Fear, Shame and Hypocrisy Around Money
I started to inspect my own money story closely and was astounded at what I found! I realized I felt fear and shame around money. I even discovered an appalling cynicism as I saw how much I worked, because I wanted to earn more money in my business, but then I kept on insisting money was not important to me.

The fear I felt came from another place. I believed that if I had more money, I was going to become a bad person. I was afraid that money would corrupt me and I'd fall prey to greed and covetousness and would lose my relationship to God.

This contradiction in my money story made me feel ashamed. On the one hand I talked with passion about what I was doing, but on the other hand I didn't like telling people I had a business, because I myself had ascribed a negative connotation to the pursuit of wealth.

Looking at the people around me I discovered I wasn't the only one with this contradictory approach to money. I could clearly see that regarding the pursuit of money as shamefully unspiritual caused many people who honestly wanted to make a good living to feel fear and shame around their prosperity. This led to a cynical lifestyle wherein they devoted huge amounts of their time and energy to creating wealth, but, at the same time, tried to play down their achievements out of a sense of shame and guilt for being prosperous.

Digging even deeper, I found several symptoms that revealed a bad relationship to money, within myself and inside of others:

Seven Symptoms of a Bad Relationship with Money:

1. Not Taking Responsibility for Your Financial Life
Many people have a victim mentality when it comes to money. They believe life just happens to them and they are the victim of their circumstances. If they are not happy with their situation, they blame it on their past, on another person or on the government. They don't believe they sit at the steering wheel of their own life.

2. No Apparent Goals
Many people just "do" life, with no specific financial goals in mind, other than paying their bills, spending on things or possibly saving up for their future. When asked if they want to earn more money, they'll probably say "yes." But most of them won't know how much they want or specifically what they would do with a higher income, other than spend it on a new car or a vacation and then go right back to the current level of income they're used to. You can see they don't have a place for money in their lives, because they don't have a specific plan

for a higher level of income. They're financially aimless, with no goals and no commitment.

3. A Negative Money Mindset

Most people have a lot of anxiety around money and tend to have a negative perspective on the world. In their eyes, there just isn't enough money to go around and they're lucky if they can get some of it. Expecting things to go wrong with money they often don't even contemplate the possibility of improving their financial situation, even if the doors of opportunity open.

4. Resentment About Other People's Wealth

Ask yourself: what do you think when a rich man stops beside you in his latest model luxury car at a red light? Whatever you think of him will determine your own level of income! If you resent well-to-do people because you think they're superficial and only got rich at the expense of others, then you'll probably never get rich, because, indirectly, you're despising money and what it brings about in other people's lives.

5. Feelings of Unworthiness

Most people inherently think they're not a good enough person and are therefore undeserving of receiving good things, including prosperity. They manifest their bad relationship with money by not expecting to attain it, instead of believing in their value and opening their arms to embrace wealth as part of their lives.

6. Connecting More Money with Hard Work

Due to our educational system, we're taught to believe we can only earn more money by working harder. That means that, in your subconscious mind, whenever you want—or need—to increase your income, you immediately think of having to work much harder and for longer hours.

By associating having more money with more work and less time, you will tend to settle for a given level of income you feel you have diligently worked "enough" for.

7. Believing a Good Academic Education is Enough

Many people value their education and academic achievements so much they think they've reached the pinnacle of knowledge and don't need to learn anything more. This is intellectual snobbism. Just because you have a master's degree or a PhD in something does not mean you don't have to learn to manage your money well. The truth is, if you are not as successful about money as you would like to be, there is something you don't know about money that you still have to learn.

The Effects of a Bad Relationship with Money

It breaks my heart to see how many women have a bad relationship with money. Ignorance, wrong beliefs and fear around money are rampant in the feminine business world.

They might recognize the importance of being savvy with money when it comes to their jobs or businesses, or even their future plans, but they tend to ignore it when it comes to challenges they face in their marriage, family, children, friends, health and personal fulfillment. They fail to recognize the true importance finances really have in these areas.

As stated earlier, money affects your life much more than you think! I can assure you that even while you read these pages, you will probably have some kind of situation going on in your life that is either directly or indirectly related to money.

Be it emotional, mental or physical stress, family problems or even problems in your marriage, money and the way you relate to it—directly or indirectly—is probably more often than not the root of the problem.

Believe me, there is nothing spiritual about ignoring the importance of wealth in your life. If you choose to do so, you will not be able to thrive in a godly way, either in your business or in your life!

No wonder Jesus taught so much about money in the Bible! Much more than He did about prayer or any other subject that is considered to be "more spiritual" than money! He knew we had to relate properly to it to live a balanced life.

Wealth Creation is Spiritual

In the Bible it clearly states that prosperity is not only spiritual, but highly desired by God for his people. He is the ultimate Entrepreneur, the Creator and we are made in His image.

This is clearly seen in how Jews, God's people from the Old Testament, relate to money. Historically, the Jewish people have shown themselves to be very good at not only handling, but also at multiplying money. The Jewish business genius is due to the fact that Judaism's spiritual regimen allows for a guilt-free appreciation of wealth accumulation.

The Old Testament, which we share with the Jewish religion, is full of examples and teachings clearly showing how God made His chosen people prosper many times in miraculous ways. Prosperity was always the direct effect of a blessing, whereas lack and need had an unequivocal negative connotation.

A good example is in chapter 28 of the *Book of Deuteronomy*, in which God describes the blessings His people will receive if they follow His commandments from verse 1 to 14. In these verses He promises supernatural enrichment and wellbeing for their bodies, their belongings and every project they undertake, including freedom from debt and protection from their enemies:

> "Now it shall come to pass, if you diligently obey the voice of the Lord your God, to observe carefully all His commandments

which I command you today, that the Lord your God will set you high above all nations of the earth. And all these blessings shall come upon you and overtake you, because you obey the voice of the Lord your God:

Blessed shall you be in the city, and blessed shall you be in the country.

Blessed shall be the fruit of your body, the produce of your ground and the increase of your herds, the increase of your cattle and the offspring of your flocks.

Blessed shall be your basket and your kneading bowl.

Blessed shall you be when you come in, and blessed shall you be when you go out.

The Lord will cause your enemies who rise against you to be defeated before your face; they shall come out against you one way and flee before you seven ways.

The Lord will command the blessing on you in your storehouses and in all to which you set your hand, and He will bless you in the land which the Lord your God is giving you.

The Lord will establish you as a holy people to Himself, just as He has sworn to you, if you keep the commandments of the Lord your God and walk in His ways. Then all peoples of the earth shall see that you are called by the name of the Lord, and they shall be afraid of you.

And the Lord will grant you plenty of goods, in the fruit of your body, in the increase of your livestock, and in the produce of your ground, in the land of which the Lord swore to your fathers to give you.

The Lord will open to you His good treasure, the heavens, to give the rain to your land in its season, and to bless all the work of your hand. You shall lend to many nations, but you shall not borrow. And the Lord will make you the head and not the tail; you shall be above only, and not be beneath, if you heed the commandments of the Lord your God, which I command you today, and are careful to observe them. So you shall not turn aside from any of the words which I command you this day, to the right or the left, to go after other gods to serve them."

– *Deuteronomy* 28:1-14, New King James Version (NKJV)

The rest of this chapter refers to what they will receive if they turn their back on Him. It's a long list of curses, sicknesses and maladies expressing that God clearly doesn't favor them.

Although this might sound obvious, in many Christian circles it's believed God will cause sickness and poverty to teach people a lesson about something. They deduct that "it must have been God" when they witness how people overcome difficulties and become spiritually stronger because of a crisis in their lives.

That's just as ridiculous as deducing that all highway accidents are caused by ambulance drivers, policemen and firefighters, because they always show up when there's a car crash!

God is life-giving, loving and rewarding by nature. He loves you passionately and will never harm you in order to teach you something, in the same way you would never let your child burn his hand on a stove so she/he learned not to touch hot ovens!

Let's face it: most bad things that financially happen to us are out of ignorance or bad decisions—or just because stuff happens. We're part of a fallen system in which a lot of people make bad decisions that can also affect our lives.

The good thing is that God will always be there to help and strengthen you. He will give you the wisdom to overcome any situation and even provide supernaturally to cover all of your needs!

"And my God shall supply all your need according to His riches in glory by Christ Jesus."

> – *Philippians* 4: 19, New King James Version.

Money, the Root of All Evil?

In the Christian belief system, misconceptions about money and its evil power have their roots in religious principles that originated in the poverty vows made by Catholic monks during medieval times. Additionally, many passages in the Bible around money have been misinterpreted or taken out of context. The sad result is it's taught in Christian circles that everything having to do with money is to be avoided, leading to the commonplace, negative manner with which people approach "filthy lucre" in the Western hemisphere.

Money is NOT the root of all evil. The Bible clearly states that it is the LOVE of money that is the root of all evil:

"For the love of money is a root of all kinds of evil, for which some have strayed from the faith in their greediness, and pierced themselves through with many sorrows".

> – 1 *Timothy* 6:15.

Being a businesswoman on top of her numbers, pursuing wealth does not mean you love money like a God or have become covetous. It means you're a good steward of the resources God has given you!

If you have had the same fear I had of becoming a bad person by pursuing money, then it is vitally important that you understand that following wealth through a business is not only spiritual; it is highly beneficial for your personal development, which will directly affect your family and community, even your nation!

What would become of any economy if it were not for courageous businesspeople who open companies that give jobs to millions and keep the economy running? If you are called to the business world, it's an honorable position, equal to any other calling God may give to humankind. You have the privilege of blessing others through a thriving business that gives life to your nation!

Don't be afraid of stepping fully into that calling and the success that comes with it! Just as you might encounter fear of failing, it can very often be fear of succeeding that may hold you back.

Rest assured, you won't turn into a bad person if you have more money. Money does not have the power to change you; it will only magnify what you already are. If you're a generous person, you will be able to be much more generous once you have more money and vice versa.

It's also not necessary that you be cynical or feel shame if you do have more money than others. If the people around you have problems with your prosperity, it's their issue, not yours. Surround yourself with people who understand your vision and who encourage you to earn more income through what you love doing.

If God called you to the marketplace and gave you the talents to multiply money through your business, go for it! He does not have any problems with that; on the contrary, He delights in your prosperity!

"Let them shout for joy and be glad,
Who favor my righteous cause;
And let them say continually,
'Let the Lord be magnified,
Who has pleasure in the prosperity of His servant.'"

— Psalm 35:27.

Summary Chapter 11: The Wealthy Queen—
The Businesswoman and Her Money

- Most women have a bad relationship with money, because they were taught to believe that money and the pursuit of it is not acceptable.

- The result is that they cultivate a bad relationship with money, because they choose to deny the importance that money has in their lives. They compartmentalize their personal finances, separating this from all other areas of life.

- We love to say that money is not important, but the truth is, it touches every single area of our life! And because it is intimately connected to every aspect of our lives, money should be given the place of importance and respect it deserves to have.

- There is nothing spiritual about ignoring the importance of wealth in your life. If you choose to do so, you will not be able to thrive in a godly way, either in your business or in your life!

- The Old Testament is full of examples and teachings that clearly show how God made His chosen people prosper many times in miraculous ways. Prosperity was always the direct effect of a blessing, whereas lack and need had an unequivocal negative connotation.

- Being a businesswoman on top of her numbers, pursuing wealth does not mean you love money like a God or have become covetous. It means you're a good steward of the resources God has given you!

- Money does not have the power to change you; it will only magnify what you already are. If you're a generous person, you will be able to be much more generous once you have more money and vice versa.

Powerful Action Step:

Discover which limiting beliefs around money are holding you back and journal about how you can replace them with new beliefs that will help you prosper from now on. (You can find examples of the most common limiting money beliefs in my complimentary workbook at www.TheQueensWorkbook.com)

Chapter 12

THE OVERCOMING QUEEN

How to Heal Your Money Story

M iriam quickly shoved the bread into the oven. Just in time to get ready for tonight's Bible study at the pastor's house! He held weekly meetings at his home for people who wanted to learn more about the Word of God.

Miriam always enjoyed these meetings. She loved God with all her heart and found her joy and peace by listening to His Word, worshipping Him and having fellowship with other Christians. Today was going to be extra special, because a visiting minister was going to teach.

As the whole family bustled into the car, she noticed Miguel was quiet and troubled. On their way to the pastor's house, he told her about the problems he was encountering at work. Miriam tried to cheer him up by telling her about Giovanna's visit, but Miguel only got mad when she informed him about the new leak in the roof.

She realized he had not been his usual happy self lately. When they first moved into their new home in the countryside, they had been joyful because of their newfound sense of freedom. Living a simpler life in touch with nature, without rushing to their jobs every day or constantly fearing Sandra's asthma attacks was liberating indeed.

Previously they had a large amount of savings in the bank, but had to spend a big portion of it on repairs for their new home. Their expectations of earning enough money to live here were much higher than had turned out to be the case. Miguel's job barely paid the bills and her gluten-free baking only generated a significant cash flow during the high tourist season. She remembered how exhausted she'd feel after spending the whole day baking in the kitchen during the hot summer months.

But Miriam also recalled how she had resolved to be strong during these challenging moments. Who said that this change was going to be easy? Besides, their former life had not been much better, except for their financial situation, which had obviously deteriorated after leaving their high paying jobs. But they had counted on that. Didn't they decide to renounce their high standard of living to seek out a more peaceful lifestyle?

But suddenly their idyllic life was not that attractive anymore. Miriam realized she had tried to deny Miguel's and her discontent for the last few months. She just did not want to admit they had been wrong! But, after Giovanna's buoyant visit and the feelings that had arisen in her whilst listening to her detailed account of their trip to Italy, the nagging suspicion that they had somehow missed something was becoming more and more evident to her.

Up to this point she had always thought that money was not important to her and had even been proud of Miguel's and her decision to relinquish their high standard of living in search of a more spiritual and fulfilling lifestyle. But had this really brought them the happiness they'd been looking for?

A bump in the road brought her back to reality. They had arrived… and were late! Miriam quickly got out of the car and followed Miguel and the children into their pastor's home. As usual, they were received affectionately by his wife, who offered them a warm drink and escorted them to the living room.

The Bible study had already started, so they quickly took their places beside a cozy fireside and opened their Bibles. Miriam scarcely noticed the visitor who was teaching. She still was deeply disturbed about the thoughts she'd entertained in the car. Tears were starting to fill her eyes as she sensed how her hope for a new and better life was evaporating. If the decision of leaving the city and moving to the countryside had been wrong, what was left for them? What would they do now?

"Are you tired? Worn out? Burned out on religion? Come to me. Get away with me and you'll recover your life. I'll show you how to take a real rest. Walk with me and work with me—watch how I do it. Learn the unforced rhythms of grace. I won't lay anything heavy or ill-fitting on you. Keep company with me and you'll learn to live freely and lightly."

– *Matthew* 11:28-30, *The Message Bible.*

The words rang in Miriam's ears. Tired and worn out? Yes, that was exactly what she was feeling right now! Tired of trying to pursue a freedom that only eluded them and worn out from never being able to find it. She fixed her eyes on the teaching minister. He was quite young and very slim. But there was something different about him that she had never seen before. This man preached from the Bible with fervor and authority.

He was catching her attention. She could not help noticing how powerful the words were proclaimed from his mouth. She quickly opened her Bible to follow his teachings:

"Do not be conformed to this world (this age), [fashioned after and adapted to its external, superficial customs], but be transformed (changed) by the [entire] renewal of your mind [by its new ideals and its new attitude], so that you may prove [for yourselves] what is the good and acceptable and perfect will of God, even the thing which is good and acceptable and perfect [in His sight for you]."

— *Romans* 12:2, *Amplified Bible* (AMP).

These words sunk into Miriam's heart. She knew this message was directly from God to her! For the rest of the meeting she attentively absorbed every word that came from this teacher's mouth, like a sponge. He talked about how God had already provided all our needs; mental, spiritual, physical, relational and financial, but that it was necessary for us to adopt a different way of thinking.

"For as a man thinks in his heart, so is he."

— *Proverbs* 23:7, New King James Version.

The way we believe or think about God in our relationship with Him controls the way we view and relate to ourselves and how we'll view and relate to others and material things, including money.

Most people, including Christians, relate to God through guilt and/or obligation. They are oblivious to God's promise and to how we can access each and every one of them through his grace, not by our own efforts to please him or achieve our goals. We perceive what is true for our lives through the five physical senses, which leads us to doubt anything we can't see, hear, feel, smell or touch.

Once we change our way of thinking and adopt God's Word as our truth, even if we cannot see it, then we open ourselves to receive His unconditional love. Then the change inside will start manifesting His promises, that He has already freely given us, in our natural lives as well.

"This is too good to be true!" Miriam thought.

"And this is the 'too good to be true' Gospel", the minister said and closed his Bible.

Miriam gasped. God was reading her mind! Tears filled her eyes again, but this time they were teardrops of gratitude. How faithful God was! In her darkest moments He always showed up somehow to restore her hope again.

She looked at Miguel. As he smiled back at her she knew that he had been deeply touched too. His whole countenance had changed!

On their way home they shared their new revelation of how God loved them unconditionally, had already met all their needs and how they had to renew their minds to believe differently than they had up to this point. They were excited and relieved. It was as if they had fallen in love with God all over again!

Now they knew there was a way to live a fulfilled life without living in need and they fully trusted God would show them how this new way of approaching their relationship to Him would also affect every other area of their lives as well.

"But seek first the kingdom of God and His righteousness, and all these things shall be added to you."
        – *Matthew* 6:33, New King James Version.

What Are Your Core Beliefs Around Money?

If you are a woman entrepreneur and any of the following situations describe you, rest assured: you can dramatically improve your income level, just by changing your beliefs around money!

- You cannot earn more money, even if you work harder. You are exhausted and have lost your motivation for what you do, because you are taking care of everybody else, except of yourself.
- You suffer under "money-hypocrisy." Although you think "money shouldn't matter," you keep on worrying about money and about how to pay your bills.
- You do have enough money, but you spend it all and feel guilty, because you have a hard time saving money.
- You are afraid of your future and don't trust money will be there for you when you need it.
- You tend to avoid talking about money with family, clients, the bank or whoever, because it makes you feel uncomfortable.

If one or more of these situations describes you, then you can prepare yourself for a powerful money makeover, because you don't have to keep on relating so negatively to your money. You can change that story!

The most powerful way to get your money story straight is by going right back to where it started: your childhood.

In coaching women about money, I have found that all of them have, in some way or other, made a silent agreement with themselves or with another person about how they view money, when they were very young.

This silent agreement is very often made to protect themselves from harm or to fill a deep need they feel in that moment. Later on, in their adult lives, this silent agreement does not serve them anymore, but it still governs their belief system and causes them to get stuck when they pursue financial growth.

One very good example is Valentina, one of my clients, whom I helped to discover that her authoritative father made her believe, when she was little, that she would never be able to reach his standards. As an adult and brilliant coach, she kept on believing that she did not perform well enough as a coach, so she undercharged the fees for her services.

Once she made this connection and was led through a healing process relating to her past, she could quickly connect with her true worth and confidently charge a new level of fees that were previously unthinkable for her.

After this root of the problem is taken care of, there is still a vast field of practical money management that has to be learnt.

In my experience as a businesswoman, I have seen that many personal finance courses crafted by men are more difficult to implement by women. This is because women are much more susceptible to succumbing to inner conflicts around money. They need to eliminate emotional triggers such as guilt, shame or blame from their life before feeling free to take aligned action in their personal and business finances.

Before they can change anything, they need to discover and acknowledge their unique money strengths and gifts, along with their money shadow-side that has always led them to repeat the same mistakes regarding wealth, over and over again.

In my opinion, one of the best approaches that can help you experience a solid change in your money story is the "Sacred Money Archetypes" method developed by Kendall Summerhawk.

I have successfully used my archetypes to leverage my money strengths into a higher achievement level, without trying to fit into a box of "what I should do" with my money matters. It helped me change the way I related to money and led me to become a Certified Coach in this method, because I knew it would also help my clients overcome their money challenges.

This method is so powerful because it considers the personality traits of each person and helps them design life-changing money habits without violating the individuality of each woman.

To me, one of the most beautiful parts of this work is that it is devoid of judgment. None of the archetypes are "incapable" or more capable of making money. All of them have the necessary attributes to help you prosper in life, which makes perfect sense with what the Bible teaches about us:

"For we are God's [own] handiwork (His workmanship), recreated in Christ Jesus, [born anew] that we may do those good works which God predestined (planned beforehand) for us [taking paths which He prepared ahead of time], that we should walk in them [living the good life which He prearranged and made ready for us to live]."

– *Ephesians* 2:10, *Amplified Bible* (AMP).

The word "handiwork" comes from the original Greek word "poiema," from which the English word for poem is derived. It actually means a wonderful work of art, or a "masterpiece."

God has given us a perfect combination of talents and abilities to triumph in life. He has fashioned us for greatness and has even designed an exciting and perfect plan for our lives!

Dear Entrepreneurial woman, you are God's masterpiece, you were designed to live an extraordinary life.

And you will need to be good friends with your money to make it happen!

Don't let any wrong beliefs about money ever deter you from living the good life God has already prepared for you!

Powerful Money Lessons from God

I myself set out to undertake a profound and prayerful quest for God's Truth around money, by studying every verse that talks about prosperity, gold, abundance, riches, need, lack, money, supply, labor, wealth, treasure, etc.

My certainty was the same I had when I studied the virtuous woman and how to educate our children, based on *Colossians* 2:2 and 3:

"...both of the Father and of Christ, in whom are hidden all the treasures of wisdom and knowledge."

Just as He had done before, I knew God would shed new light on the Truth about money and wealth. I had already heard a lot of teachings about prosperity and money, but I wanted to dig deeper, so I asked God to give me a revelation that would give me a deep conviction I could run with.

It is beyond the scope of this book to give an exhaustive teaching about Biblical finances—there are already a lot of very good resources about that. But I do want to share with you the most important revelations God has given me personally around money.

They are all rooted around the simple fact that God did not create us to bear the burden of our provision and of our life, for that matter. As much as you would like to believe it, your human brain was not designed to be the sole entity responsible for governing your life by itself.

We were intricately designed by our Creator to live our life united with God Himself, through a strong, spiritual connection from which we can draw the wisdom, strength and supernatural power to meet all of our needs.

In the beginning, man was united to God in a perfect way. Adam and Eve had all of their needs met and they never had to stress out about not having food, time, being unfulfilled or not having a meaning for their lives.

Then they lost that connection and the problems started. Suddenly they were "their own gods," determined to live their lives by themselves, disconnected from God. And that is why humankind has failed miserably to reach happiness and fulfillment in a perpetual way, throughout the whole of human history until now. We just can't accomplish it on our own!

Most of us are taught to believe we can and should educate our brains so we can take responsibility for ourselves. Take a look around you. How has that worked for you and for others?

I'm in no way demeaning our intellectual capabilities. God gave them to us and we need to educate ourselves. If I fly in an airplane, I would like the pilot to know how to fly it! But I would also like him to be able to divinely discern if something is wrong with the plane or how to maneuver it out of a potential disaster with superhuman wisdom.

Very often called "sixth sense" or intuition, this is a remnant of a state of mind God originally intended for us to live in permanently. He created us with the ability to operate beyond our five physical senses.

In your life you have most probably experienced a sense, or a feeling about something that was not logical, but you knew it was true. You had a "hunch" about something, maybe even your business.

The problem is that most of us operate in a very rudimentary state of spiritual awareness, because we were never educated to develop it any further. But this does not have to stay that way!

The Bible says that, as children of God, we are led by the Spirit of God, according to *Romans* 8:14 (New King James Version):

"For as many as are led by the Spirit of God, these are sons of God".

Imagine if you could go back to that God-connection and the original state of perception God created you with! You would be able to constantly tap into His wisdom and knowledge about everything in your life!

The Good News

The good news is that God did not design a plan "B" to help us fix our fallen condition, but sent His own son, Jesus Christ, to redeem us and to restore our original state of intimate connection to God. Every person that accepts that gift by faith in the work of Jesus can confidently step into a vibrating, exciting and personal relationship with God again.

Once that happens, it will affect the way you run your whole life. You won't have to rely on your own, limited ability to live your life anymore, but can now draw upon God's immeasurable wisdom and grace for provision for all of your needs!

God promises to guide us in our business ventures:

"Thus says the Lord, your Redeemer,
The Holy One of Israel:
'I am the Lord your God,
Who teaches you to profit,
Who leads you by the way you should go.'"
– *Isaiah* 48:17, New King James Version.

You can open yourself to God's guidance and start operating in a thriving, heavenly economy that never suffers under recession or lack in any way. It is not founded on logical reasoning, but on supernatural provision. It is God's way of doing math!

These are the most important principles that govern God's economy:

1. God is Your Source

In a personal relationship with a loving and faithful God as your father, you do not have to carry the burden of providing for yourself anymore. You can become assignment-minded, instead of being provision-minded. That means you can freely focus on fulfilling your calling to your business, drawing from the grace of God, instead of making decisions to provide for yourself.

This does not mean you can throw your brains out of the window. Do your homework and give it your best, but don't carry the burden of your provision. Trust in God. He will guide you in the way you can prosper and even provide for you supernaturally. Maybe not in the way you think He should, but He will take good care of you!

2. Generosity: The More You Give, the More You Get

One of the most powerful concepts for financial success God's way is the act of giving. Although it defies all human logic, in God's economy, you get more when you give more. It is actually a law that is so effective that even non-Christian business people apply it to their businesses. They know they earn more if they give or "tithe" a portion of their revenue.

You can view yourself as a river, through which a lot of money flows. The bigger the quantity of money that flows out, the bigger the amount that comes in. Compare it to stagnant water: it does not flow anywhere, there is no continuous replenishment and it usually stinks!

3. Detachment: There is Always Enough Money, So Don't Stress Over It

This is one of the most impactful revelations God gave me around money, years ago. I asked Him to reveal to me why Jesus, who said that, "He who has seen me has seen the Father" (*John* 14:9), was seemingly indifferent to money.

On the one hand I myself was trying to get rid of my "money is not important" mentality, because I could clearly see that God does not want us to be ignorant about it and desires to see us prosperous. Jesus Himself taught us to be good stewards of our money!

But then, when I went to the Scriptures and read about Jesus' life, I did not get the impression of Him being particularly "money friendly."

On the contrary, he violently drove the merchants and money changers out of the temple, claiming that God's holy place was a house of prayer, not a den of thieves (*Matthew* 21:13). He told us to be careful of turning money into our God (*Luke* 16:13) and clearly challenged a rich, young ruler regarding his wealth (*Mark* 10:23-25).

In my eyes, Jesus was more against than in favor of money! How could I reconcile this attitude with the revelation God had given me of the prosperous, money savvy virtuous woman He had called me to become?

The answer is detachment. Detachment from money. Jesus was not against money, but warned us not to be attached to it, or trust in it, instead of fully trusting in God. He understood how Godly prosperity and supernatural provision really work and was fully focused on His mission, knowing that the Lord's infinite ability to provide was available whenever He needed it. Jesus was so sure about God's abundant provision for His life, that He could feed 5,000 people with five loaves of bread and two fishes, without having to figure out how that works. To pay his taxes he sent Peter to catch a fish that had swallowed a coin.

Wow, imagine if you could reach such a state of perception of the divine provision that is already available to you, for yourself, your family and your business!

While this may seem too extreme for our brain, there is a lesson here! This is not a place where we can wash down the Bible by resigning ourselves with by saying: "yeah, but that was Jesus"! God said we should—and could—walk as Jesus did!

> "He who says he abides in Him ought himself also to walk just as He walked."
>
> – 1 *John* 2:6, New King James Version.

Our education has hardened our hearts from receiving a form of provision only very few humans have ever learned to operate in. This realm is so foreign to us because we have focused too much on developing our brain instead of our spiritual God-given ability to transcend the material realm and see beyond what we can touch, see, smell or hear.

Nevertheless, it does not have to stay that way! Maybe you are not ready to catch a fish to pay your taxes, but you can rest in God when you encounter financial difficulties and open your mind to His teachings, so that your humanistic thinking can be transformed and your mind can open itself to receiving miracles from God, instead of trying to figure everything out with your limited human brain.

You can learn to operate in the spiritual realm. You were created to do so! So, start connecting to God first.

Jesus said: "I am the way, the truth, and the life. No one comes to the Father except through Me."

– John 14:6.

By accepting the finished work of Jesus on the cross, where He paid for your sins that were separating you from God, you will reestablish your original relationship to God.

According to *Romans* 10:8-10, New King James Version: "But what does it say? The word is near you, in your mouth and in your heart: that is, the word of faith which we preach; That if you confess with your mouth the Lord Jesus and believe in your heart that God has raised Him from the dead, you will be saved. For with the heart one believes unto righteousness, and with the mouth confession is made unto salvation."

A Powerful Spiritual Journey in Intimate Relationship with God Himself

Once you have made this step of accepting Jesus as your Lord and Savior, God's Holy Spirit will come to live in you and reveal God and his wisdom to you.

– 1 *Corinthians* 2:6-16, New King James Version, proclaims:

"However, we speak wisdom among those who are mature, yet not the wisdom of this age, nor of the rulers of this age, who are coming to nothing; But we speak the wisdom of God in a mystery, the hidden wisdom which God ordained before the ages for our glory; which none of the rulers of this age knew; for had they known, they would not have crucified the Lord of glory. But as it is written:

"Eye has not seen, nor ear heard, Nor have entered into the heart of man, The things which God has prepared for those who love Him."

"But God has revealed them to us through His Spirit: For the Spirit searches all things, yes, the deep things of God. For what man knows the things of a man except the spirit of the man which is in him? Even so no one knows the things of God except the Spirit of God. Now we have received, not the spirit of the world, but the Spirit who is from God, that we might know the things that have been freely given to us by God".

Now you can start your own powerful spiritual journey in intimate relationship with God Himself, who will teach you to operate with money according to His Truth. He will help you prepare your heart, so you can receive freely from His supernatural grace, God's amazing gift of divine ability for us!

He is passionately waiting for you to give Him permission to become part of your life and your business. He will not impose Himself on you; he is a gentleman, patiently waiting to be invited to show you a new and exciting way to live your life. But you have to surrender and then let Him change your heart first.

Because God can't take you where your heart won't let you go!

Your heart is changed as you learn more about Him and the way He operates. As you draw near to Him and His Word, you will shift your mindset about many things in your life. Healing and restoration of even impossible situations will take place, and you will discover His perfect plan for you and your loved ones!

**Summary Chapter Chapter 12: The Overcoming Queen—
How to Heal Your Money Story**

- The way we believe or think about God in our relationship with Him controls the way we view and relate to ourselves and how we'll view and relate to others and material things, including money.

- Once we change our way of thinking and adopt God's Word as our truth, even if we cannot see it, then we open ourselves to receive His unconditional love.

- Women are much more susceptible than men to succumbing to inner conflicts around money. They need to eliminate emotional triggers such as guilt, shame or blame from their life before feeling free to take aligned action in their personal and business finances.

- God has given us a perfect combination of talents and abilities to triumph in life. He has fashioned us for greatness and has even designed an exciting and perfect plan for our lives!

- We were intricately designed by our Creator to live our life united with God Himself, through a strong, spiritual connection from which we can draw the wisdom, strength and supernatural power to meet all of our needs.

- Although it defies all human logic, in God's economy, you get more when you give more.

- We have focused too much on developing our brain instead of our spiritual God-given ability to transcend the material realm and see beyond what we can touch, see, smell or hear.

Powerful Action Step:

Close your eyes.

Imagine you have all the money you need to live the life of your dreams.

What do you spend time on? What do you feel is your purpose? What impact do you focus on creating?

Be as specific as you can, and allow yourself to dream.

Read Matthew 6:25-35 and ask yourself:

What would your life look like if you would adopt this belief as truth for your life?

What would your income look like if you would adopt this belief as truth for your business?

AFTERWORD

God Loves You, But You Have a Part to Play!

Before closing the book, I want to share with you how my very own spiritual journey started:

It was back in 1993. Our third child had been born a few months earlier and I was an emotional wreck. On the outside I was a proud mom and happily married young woman, but inside I was confronting chapters of my traumatic childhood that I had never addressed before. I felt unable to face the task of raising our three children and desperately needed help.

In my quest for meaning and hope for my life I started attending a Bible study group. At first it was just another way to socially gather with women, but soon I met one lady who was very different than the others. She talked about a personal relationship with God. Every time she shared from her life it seemed that she knew Jesus, as if He were her personal friend.

Although I had been brought up in a religious home and had gone to church every now and then, I had never heard anybody talk about God in that way before.

I was instantly attracted to this lady. She had an aura of inner peace and godly kindness that was irresistible to my tormented soul. I wanted what she had!

One day she told me about how she made a decision to accept Jesus as her Savior. She called it being born again and read to me the story of Nicodemus, who secretly sought Jesus out at night, to find out how to access God. You can find this story in *The Book of John*, 3: 1-7.

"There was a man of the Pharisees named Nicodemus, a ruler of the Jews. This man came to Jesus by night and said to Him, 'Rabbi, we know that You are a teacher come from God; for no one can do these signs that You do unless God is with him.'

"Jesus answered and said to him, 'Most assuredly, I say to you, unless one is born again, he cannot see the kingdom of God.'

"Nicodemus said to Him, 'How can a man be born when he is old? Can he enter a second time into his mother's womb and be born?'

"Jesus answered, 'Most assuredly, I say to you, unless one is born of water and the Spirit, he cannot enter the kingdom of God. That which is born of the flesh is flesh, and that which is born of the Spirit is spirit. Do not marvel that I said to you, 'You must be born again.'"

– (*John* 3:1-7)

That day I understood why I had not experienced an authentic connection to God.

Just like Nicodemus, I had been a religious person, but had never made a conscious decision to accept Jesus into my life. This lady explained to me that although God loved each and every human being on this planet, He had given us the freedom to choose to be partakers of the blessings Jesus purchased for us on the cross.

She explained to me how Jesus died on the cross to pay for my sins, to set me free to become part of God's family. Then she invited me to give my life to Jesus and helped me pray a prayer of salvation. Although I did not fully realize the magnitude of what happened in the spiritual realm back then, I now fully realize that I made the most important decision of my life that day!

I was born again and I made the God-connection! From that day onward a beautiful spiritual journey started that I am still passionately travelling on to this day. Jesus healed my past and filled me with hope for the future. He has given me wisdom, counselling and comfort during all these years. Truthfully, I don't think I would have made it this far without Him!

He is the one who gave me the strength and the guidance to be a homeschooling mom and an entrepreneurial woman.

You can Choose to Participate in God's Plan for You
What I desire for you to understand is that a relationship with God does not just drop into your lap. You cannot freely enjoy fellowshipping intimately with Him unless you decide to invite Him into your life.

It is a conscious decision every person that wants to make a God-connection has to make. That is the ultimate freedom our loving father God gave us: The freedom to choose whether or not we would accept Him in our lives.

Dear entrepreneurial woman, maybe you can identify with my story and you yearn to be connected to God. Maybe you feel like a sleeping queen who has an awesome calling for her life but who doesn't dare to wake up, because it scares you to death and you feel totally incapable of ever making it happen?

Rest assured, you can count on God's guidance to walk in that amazing life he has revealed to you in your heart and that goes beyond your wildest dreams!

If you have never accepted Jesus in your life you can choose to walk with God and accept the offer He is making to you today: Come to the cross of Jesus, lay down your shadow story and step into a new blessed and guilt-free life by becoming part of His family!

If you confess with your mouth to the Lord Jesus and believe in your heart that God has raised him from the dead, you will be saved. "For with the heart one believes unto righteousness, and with the mouth confession is made unto salvation." (*Romans* 10:9, 10)

I invite you to voice your decision with the following prayer:

PRAYER

Dear Lord Jesus,

I want to live with You. I need Your mercy to forgive me and I need Your grace to change me. Thank You for Your amazing, unconditional love. Thank You for giving me life and eternity. Thank You for dying on the cross for me.

I accept You as my Lord and Savior. Now I'm a Christian, which means You live in me. I belong to You now… Amen.

ABOUT THE AUTHOR

Bettina Langerfeldt has been happily married to her husband Robert, since 1986. They live in Chile and have four children, whom they homeschooled with a methodology that fostered their entrepreneurial and leadership skills.

This experience led her to start her own entrepreneurial faith-journey, a challenging path which forced her to question her own beliefs around the spirituality of money, business and godly entrepreneurship.

In 2007, Bettina started sharing her experience through a successful online business in the Spanish market. She is an author, lecturer, coach and web business strategist. Now she's taking her inspiring message and expertise to Christian women worldwide.

You can contact Bettina or find out more about her and her products and services at www.BettinaLangerfeldt.com . You can also follow her on her Fan Page in Facebook, at www.facebook.com/bettina.en

BONUS OFFER

Are you ready to awaken to your God-given potential as a female leader and business woman queen?

Simply go to:
www.TheQueensWorkbook.com
and sign up for Bettina's free workbook: **"The Sleeping Queen's Workbook for Business Women"** that will help you apply the

principles you learned in this book to your finances, your business, and your personal life.

You will receive:

- Practical exercises that will help you improve your relationship with money.
- Powerful money breakthroughs with Bettina's insightful coaching questions.
- New revelations of the plan of God for your business and your life.
- Valuable business tips that will refresh the way you see your niche, your team, your services, your visibility and your marketing.
- Empowering mindset shifts as you learn how to reframe limiting beliefs that have held you back from stepping into your full potential as a godly business woman.

INDEX